F
ſ

E

I SURVIVED THE
SOMME

This book is made up of a selection of the diaries, sketches and paintings made by my father, Charles Oliver Meeres, while he was serving as a second lieutenant in the Royal Field Artillery on the Western Front between 1915 and 1918. The full collection of his work has been deposited in the Imperial War Museum.

The book is dedicated to the memory of my father, and of my mother, Margaret Lydia Meeres.

Frank Meeres

I SURVIVED THE SOMME

THE SECRET DIARY OF A TOMMY

CHARLES MEERES

EDITED BY FRANK MEERES

AMBERLEY

Cover illustration, front: British front-line trench April 1916. Courtesy of Jonathan Reeve JR2530b119fp43B 19141918.

First published in 2013

Amberley Publishing
The Hill, Stroud
Gloucestershire, GL5 4EP

www.amberley-books.com

© Text and illustrations The Estate of Charles Meeres 2013

The right of Charles Meeres to be identified as the Author of this work has been asserted in accordance with the Copyrights, Designs and Patents Act 1988.

ISBN 978 1 4456 0618 7

British Library Cataloguing in Publication Data. A catalogue record for this book is available from the British Library.

Typeset in 11pt on 16pt Palatino.
Typesetting and Origination by Amberley Publishing
Printed in the UK.

Contents

INTRODUCTION
BY FRANK MEERES

Charles Meeres was born in 1896, the son of an army officer. He chose the artillery as a career and was trained at Woolwich. While he was there, on 4 August 1914, the First World War broke out. Lord Kitchener called for 100,000 volunteers to join the army; within a few months over a million men had done so.

Meeres' training thus took place at the same time, and under the same conditions, as the men of Kitchener's army, even though he was actually a full-time professional soldier. He fought throughout the war with the 21st Division. Like them, his first experience of war was at the Battle of Loos in September 1915. In this battle the artillery, like the infantry, was to fail through inexperience, inadequate training and poor leadership. Meeres then took part in trench warfare at Armentières in the winter of 1915–6. Here the harsh conditions of life on the Western Front became only too real. As a gunner, Meeres played a key role in the Battle of the Somme, in the summer of 1916. A week-long artillery bombardment was supposed to destroy the German front line to allow the infantry to attack and overrun the enemy's defences. The breakthrough failed – with terrible consequences for the men of the New Army.

As the Western Front settled back into deadlock, the Germans rationalised their defensive front by retreating a few miles to an enormously strong defensive system, called by the Allies the Hindenburg Line. The Allies attempted to break through this line at Arras in April 1917. The attempt was a failure and the casualties as great as at the Somme. Meeres was invalided home for several months after Arras, and missed the even greater horrors of the Third Battle of Ypres. He records the impressions of the battle given to him by his fellow officers when he returned to the front.

The character of the war changed completely in the spring of 1918. On the one hand, the collapse of Russia had freed up many thousands of German soldiers from the Eastern Front. On the other, the entry of America into the war meant that the Allies would have many more soldiers themselves, once the Americans arrived on the Western Front in large numbers. In effect, the Germans had a few months to exploit their temporary numerical advantage and make a decisive breakthrough. They launched a whole series of attacks on the Western Front between March and June 1918, pushing the Allies back by up to 40 miles in some places. However, each attack ran out of steam. The Allies were able to retaliate from the end of June, pushing back the Germans. They did this at such a pace that the Germans were not even able to regroup along the Hindenburg Line. Once this line was breached, defeat was inevitable. The diaries end just a few days before the end of the war. Meeres was wounded at Poix-du-Nord on 26 October 1918.

Meeres survived the war, but was almost totally deaf for the rest of his life from the sound of the guns. He died in 1962 and is buried at Dartmouth in Devon.

The Artillery War

The impression most people have of the First World War is of infantrymen living in trenches, separated by a space known as 'No Man's Land', across which the soldiers would occasionally be ordered to attack, usually with devastating results for the attackers. In fact the infantry was only one arm of attack, the artillery was at least as important, and between 30 and 40 per cent of the men in the front line at the Western Front were in the artillery. Their story has been neglected by history: one aim of this book is to redress this injustice by telling the story of the war from the viewpoint of an artilleryman.

Artillery was the dominating force in the First World War. Artillery fire on the Western Front killed more people than rifle and machine gun fire combined: 59 per cent of wounds suffered by British soldiers were from shellfire, compared with 39 per cent from bullets. The wound was also more likely to be fatal; a man was three times more likely to die from a shell wound to the chest than from a bullet wound to the same area.

As an artilleryman, Meeres was in a rather different war than the front-line soldier, which is perhaps why he had the time and opportunity to make the drawings in this book. Malcolm Brown summed up the role of the gunner in his book, *The Imperial War Museum Book of the Western Front*: 'Artillery was generally fired from a distance "over the hill" at positions they could not see: if they could see they could be seen, and would therefore be highly vulnerable. Mathematics and map references were as much part of their armoury as shells. Not for them the heroic attack across No Man's Land, or the charge with the bayonet.' However, artillery work could be just as dangerous as the Front Line, as several entries in the diary show; if the enemy found the range, a single shell could destroy a gun and kill all the men working with it.

The First World War poet Gilbert Frankau dramatically expressed the power of the new artillery:

We are the guns, and your masters! Saw ye our flashes?
Heard ye the scream of our shells in the night, and the shuddering
crashes?
Saw ye our work at the roadside, the shrouded things lying,
Moaning to God that He made them – the maimed and the dying
Husbands or sons,
Fathers or lovers we break them. We are the guns!

The artillery was not organised into the county regiments or battalions which people associate with the war. There was one regiment – the Royal Regiment of Artillery, which was divided into three sections according to the type of weapon used. The Royal Horse Artillery manned the very light guns which worked with the cavalry; the Royal Field Artillery (RFA) manned the slightly heavier guns which worked with the infantry, while the Royal Garrison Artillery worked with the very heavy guns. Meeres was in the RFA, and his unit was attached to the 21st Division. His actual battery name changed from time to time in the war due to various reorganisations and consisted of a number of 18-pounder guns, at first four, but the number was later raised to six.

The eighteen-pounder gun had a maximum range of over 6,000 yards, but in practice on the Western Front, was usually firing at a range of 4,000 yards. Each gun was mounted in a carriage with two wooden wheels about 4 feet 6 inches in diameter. The gun was laid (placed in the right line of fire) by means of sights: normally the target was not visible to the men firing the gun, so either the position of the enemy had to be calculated from a map or someone (the Forward Observation Officer, FOO) had to go and have a look: this usually meant sharing the front-line trench with the infantry. In the days before any form of wireless communication it was difficult for him to get instructions back to the guns – telephone lines were laid, but these would very often be broken by enemy action.

The guns of a battery were normally placed in line about 20 yards apart. The limbers, wagons and horses were always kept further back, in less danger of being shelled by the enemy: this was known as the wagon-line. Where the front remained in the same place for a long time, as it did before the mobile warfare of 1918, the gun position could become very elaborate, with roofs to keep out the rain and to provide protection. Of course, the position was always vulnerable to a direct hit – or to an enemy shell coming in the open front. An enemy plane overhead often led to an attack; the plane would spot the position and communicate its location back to his own gunners. For most of the war, there was little danger of the guns being actually captured but this could occur during a rapid advance by the enemy – as Meeres describes in the spring of 1918.

The guns were pulled by horses, the back end of the gun being attached to a two-wheeled vehicle known as a 'limber'. Teams of six horses were used to pull each gun. In addition, each gun had two ammunition wagons, normally hooked together: these carried the shells in long rows of tubular baskets.

Several types of shell were in use. The most common were those containing shrapnel and those containing high explosive (HE). Shrapnel was normally used against open targets, HE against troops behind parapets and against buildings and the enemy's gun emplacements. The shell was exploded by means of a fuse (Meeres always spells this 'fuze'). These might be made to explode on hitting the target, or at a particular number of seconds after the gun was fired. One technique used against men in trenches was to 'bounce' the shell off the ground so that it was above the trench when its time-fuse caused it to explode, with deadly results for the men sheltering in the trench. Shrapnel consists of a shell containing small spherical bullets. If the shell burst too soon, these would be scattered and if it went off too late they would be buried in the ground but, if timed correctly, shrapnel was probably the most effective way of killing large numbers of advancing infantry.

Two other shells were occasionally used. The smoke shell contained a chemical which, when it was burst, would produce a quantity of smoke; the idea was to mask an advance. Gas shells fired a different sort of chemical, designed to make it hard for those being attacked to breathe; some were fatal, others caused tears and made it impossible to fight effectively.

In a bombardment, each gun normally fired at three rounds a minute (rapid fire) or four rounds a minute (intense fire). With a six-gun battery, this meant shells would be falling on the target every two and a half seconds.

Each individual gun was commanded by a sergeant called the No. 1, assisted by a corporal called the 'Coverer'. The private soldiers were either gunners, who served the guns, or drivers, who served the horses. There were about ten gunners for each gun, and about twelve drivers. There were also signallers, who worked with telephones, flags or lamps; at first they were ranked officially as either gunners or drivers, but later a separate rank of signaller was created. Junior officers, corresponding to 'lance corporals' in the infantry, were called 'Bombardiers' in the artillery. Each battery had other men in specialised tasks, such as saddlers, farriers, fitters and cooks.

Two roles are especially associated with the artillery on the Western Front. The first was the destroying of the barbed wire entanglements in front of the enemy's trenches, so that the infantry would be able to attack them. In some battles, this preliminary might take several days, but of course it did alert the enemy that an attack was planned, so later in the war it became very much shorter. Eighteen-pounder shrapnel was the most effective way of doing this, but only if the shells could be timed to burst at exactly the right place.

The other role of the artillery was to create a 'creeping barrage' – a moving curtain of shells under which the infantry might go forward. These barrages required the most elaborate preparation. In the course of one of them, a battery might have to fire about 1,000 rounds, and it might be necessary to work out the line, angle of sight and range of every round. It was also necessary to work out the number of shells of each kind – usually a mixture of shrapnel, HE and smoke – that was required, and to have them ready by each gun. The curtain or wall of shells would in fact consist of a zone of several lines of explosions. The rate of the barrage would vary according to conditions; a typical barrage might move forward 100 yards every two or three minutes.

Once a barrage had started it could be halted at a moment's notice, but it could not be slowed down or speeded up; scores, hundreds or even thousands of guns might be firing. This led to many problems; if the barrage was moving forward too slowly, the men could not advance without walking into it; if it went too fast, it left the men behind, enabling the enemy to climb onto the parapets of the trenches after the barrage had passed overhead and gun down the attackers. As the technique became more sophisticated, it was common to introduce a series of 'false starts' to a barrage to confuse the enemy: these were known as 'Chinese barrages'. Another technique was to surround a group of attacking men entirely with protective shells – a 'box' barrage.

The artillery had other roles, most commonly being engaged in counter-battery work, that is, attacking the enemy's guns. The techniques for doing this became increasingly sophisticated as the war progressed, involving flash spotting (calculating the positions of the guns from the flashes made as they fired), sound-ranging (calculating their positions from the sounds their shells made) and also working in co-operation with observers in aeroplanes.

Shells also improved in efficiency as the time passed; in 1916, Meeres was surprised by the number of unexploded shells he saw when he walked over the Somme battlefield. The greatest single advance in technology was the 106 percussion fuse for HE shells. This enabled the shell to explode immediately before it hit the ground. This had two vital effects:

1. It was much more effective in destroying barbed wire than shrapnel and meant that it was no longer necessary to spend many hours in destroying wire before an attack.
2. In a barrage it would explode without any 'backsplash', enabling the infantry to hug the barrage closer than ever before without risking their lives.

As has been said, the artillery was entirely horse-drawn, and the officers also had their own horses. The total number of horses needed was enormous – 125 for a four-gun battery and 172 for a six-gun battery. Light draught horses were preferred, where possible those that were accustomed to pulling carriages, cabs and horse-drawn trams and omnibuses. Even before 1914, the numbers of these were in decline because of the growth of motor transport, so lighter types of farm horses were also used. Mules might also be used on occasion. The finding of food and water for these animals was a constant concern; in the latter part of the war, when everything became more mobile, it also became necessary to keep them hidden to avoid an air attack.

    This, then, was the war as fought by the artilleryman.

                                                              Frank Meeres

[Note to the reader – square brackets indicate text inserted by the editor.]

THE DIARY

1
IN TRAINING

I joined the 21st Divisional Artillery at High Wycombe on 14 December 1914. I had just received my commission from the 'Shop' on 17 November, and had spent the interval in undergoing an operation for appendicitis.

We spent all our time doing drill of one sort or another. We did about six hours marching drill a day, often in the rain, always in heavy mud. Our drill-ground was Lord Lincolnshire's park on the edge of town.

Sometimes we went up to the barracks and did some 'gun-drill' on the ancient French cannon which were allotted to us for training purposes. These were 90-millimetre guns of 1880, and bore no resemblance whatever to the 18-pounders with which we should really have to fight. However, there were no 18-pounders for us to train on, so we had to make the best of what we had.

We used to drag these cumbrous engines, most of which were painted bright blue, into a swampy field below the barracks, and there we tried to practice direct laying until we were sick of it, or until it began to snow. Then we would take them up again to their yard, break off, and go home. We could not do any really useful work upon these guns, for the mechanism was entirely different from that of the 18-pounder, and moreover there were no dial-sights upon which we could practice indirect laying.

We also had riding drill. We had nine horses, which lived in different stables in the town; but we had only three sets of saddlery (or 'appointments' to use the army term), and these were of civilian type, very old, and dangerously dilapidated. The result was, that only three men could ride at a time.

The riding school was a muddy circle, often under an inch or so of water. Three horses used to go plodding and splashing round, bearing with them three wet, miserable, blue-clad drivers-to-be; while our roughrider sergeant stood on a dry patch in the middle, clad in striped trousers, a long black coat and a cloth cap, twirling his black moustaches and flourishing a stock-whip.

It was a long time before khaki uniforms were issued to the men. At first they had only their 'Kitchener' blue suits, one each; and, as the winter happened to be a very wet one, and as we drilled in all weathers, that was generally wet through. We had a few old-soldier non-commissioned officers (NCOs), and these, lacking even blue suits, appeared on parade in their own 'civvies'. A few wore oddments of old-style uniforms.

Officers and men were billeted in the town. The men of each unit were billeted as close together as possible. In our case, they all lived in a single long street, at the end of which there was an open space on which we paraded before marching off to the park or the barracks for our day's work.

At first, the officers of all the three brigades stationed at Wycombe messed at the Red Lion hotel, but later the mess of the 25th Brigade was transferred to the Falcon. We lived in billets in the town. I was billeted at a house called 'The Dhoon', upon Mrs Peace, the wife of the owner of one of the principal provision shops; and she made me extremely comfortable. At first I was alone, but later I was joined by two officers of A/95, Murray Lyon and Geddes.

By the end of March [1915], iron stables had been erected in the park and each battery had eighty or 100 horses there. The officers no longer went about on draught horses. My first charger had been an elderly 'hairy': then I acquired a small pony, which the men called Stripes on account of some curious white markings on his neck: now I was riding a handsome black charger which had been set aside originally for the Commander Royal Artillery (CRA) General Alexander, but had proved too big for him. The animal, called Ton, afterwards became White's charger, and served him throughout the War. Stripes became the trumpeter's pony, and also survived till the end of the War.

Colonel Gillson had his own method of teaching his men to ride. He used to turn the whole Brigade out with blankets only – no saddles – and lead them at a trot along the roads. At first, scores of men fell off, but after a very few days the number had greatly decreased.

Still we had only our ancient French guns, and our rifles were Snyders of 1875. But we had a certain amount of draught harness, and before long each battery possessed six more or less efficient teams. There was a big, level field above the town in which we could practice riding and driving.

Now, at last, we were really getting on.

On 25 April I was posted to the 21st Divisional Artillery Column, which was in training at Northchurch, near Berkhamsted. Early in July I was posted to C/96 battery. The battery had about eighty horses, and more arrived during the fortnight after I joined. There were no stables: the horse-lines of the whole Brigade were together in a large, level field, which we called 'Kitchener's Field'. In the middle of July we received one 18-pounder gun and eight ammunition wagons per battery.

The training of the 96th was a good deal more advanced than that of the other brigades. This was partly accounted for, no doubt, by the fact that Berkhamsted, having an extensive common, offered much greater facilities for training than High Wycombe; but it was due mainly, I am sure, to the colonel's keenness. He worked with us every day and all day. Nearly every morning he was out with one of the batteries on the common: the afternoons he spent in administrative work: in the evenings he lectured to us, or gave us ranging practice on a miniature landscape made of sand and adorned with little houses, woods, and enemy guns.

The colonel was very keen on 'drill orders'. Each battery in turn would spend a morning (and often part of an afternoon as well) on the common, practising advancing and retiring across country, dropping into action, and engaging imaginary targets. The colonel would set us tasks, and would supervise us very closely as we endeavoured to execute them. At the end, he would call us all together, go in great detail through everything that each of us had done, and distribute praise and blame. (There was generally more blame than praise!) I am sure that we learned a great deal during these mornings, and really we got a good deal of fun out of them – on those occasions, that is, when the colonel was in a good temper!

The truth is, we were all very much afraid of the colonel's temper. He had a habit of squaring the corners of his mouth so that it assumed the shape of a letter-box, and spitting out exceedingly unpleasant remarks. He treated us all like school-boys. I did not mind that particularly, as I was accustomed to that kind of treatment, having, after all, only recently left school; but some of the older men minded it very much. However, we all had a very high opinion of the colonel's ability, and, in a way, we were proud of him – and to those of whom one is proud one will forgive much.

Occasionally we had 'field days'. A field day is a bigger thing than a drill order. A drill order is a private show: in a field day, several units, and sometimes several arms, co-operate.

There was one field day when I was with 'A' battery, in which both infantry and artillery were engaged. In fact, it was more than a field day: it lasted for two days, and would have lasted for three had the weather been finer. Starting from Tring, we fought a moving battle all day, and bivouacked for the night on a heath somewhere near Dunstable. We had a miserable time, as it poured with rain, and we all got wet through. It happened that Captain White was one of the umpires. He came and fed and slept with us – whereby we gained no small advantage, for about midnight the general decided to give us a night alarm, and sent an orderly to inform the umpire; but so well had we secreted that important personage that the orderly entirely failed to find him, and so the night attack could not take place.

Another field day occurred while I was with the 96th Brigade Ammunition Column. Harrow OTC, supported by 'A' and 'B' Batteries, was pitted against the Inns of Court OTC, supported by 'C' and 'D' Batteries. My section of the column formed part of the latter force, which was under the command of Captain Keate. Our batteries took up positions about 200 yards behind the infantry; and we placed ourselves about 100 yards behind the batteries. We were drawn up on a road with our tail towards the enemy. As it turned out, this was just as well, for we were compelled to beat a rapid retreat. Our infantry and batteries retired in disorder, but for quite a long time the column, with thirty-six rifles, held the enemy at bay in the north-west corner of Ashridge Park. Finally we also retired, and the whole force withdrew to the top of a hill, where it was surrounded and compelled to surrender en bloc.

About once a week the whole Division went on a route march. Sometimes we did as much as 35 miles in the day. These marches involved, for us, a preliminary march on the preceding day to Aston Clinton, where we dined and slept as the guests of the other brigades.

We were very happy at Berkhamsted. The townspeople were very good to the men, and the latter had quite an affection for

'Berko', as they called it. It came as a blow to us when we heard that we were to be moved from Berkhamsted to the Aldershot district. We marched out of 'Berko' on 17 July. It had been raining for several days, and the harness was red with rust, and the horses and vehicles caked with mud. Despite the inclement weather, the townspeople turned out in force to bid us farewell. It was a pity that we could not look a little smarter for the occasion.

We marched through Chesham and Amersham to Wycombe Marsh, where we bivouacked for the night. The officers were accommodated at the Flackwell Heath golf club, which was neither comfortable nor cheap. On the 19th we marched to Ascot; and next day, entering the Aldershot Command, we passed through Guildford and Godalming, and came to our destination – Milford Camp.

On each of these four days Duncan went forward as billeting officer, so I had charge of his section – the left. (I had not yet a section of my own.) I was also in charge of the officers' messing arrangements. On one occasion I produced a dozen ducks' eggs for lunch. It happened that the colonel came and shared our repast, and that he was very fond of ducks' eggs – and so I advanced several points in his favour!

Milford Camp did not impress us favourably. At the moment of our arrival the whole place was a sea of mud, but afterwards this dried into red dust, which found its way onto and into everything. The officers and men lived in wooden huts. There were stables for the horses, but we could not use them at first, as they were supposed to be infected with pink-eye.

The whole of the Divisional Artillery was at Milford, and the infantry of the division was at Witley Camp, adjoining. At the end of July we all went off to Mytchett Camp to fire our musketry course at Ash ranges. This was a most depressing experience. The rain and mud proved too much for Botting, who was an elderly man. He was transferred to the Brigade

Ammunition Column, his place being taken by Lieutenant R. B. Withers.

I did not see much of Milford. During August I went to Woolwich on a short course of telephony. I returned just in time to join the battery at Larkhill, Salisbury Plain, for 'practice camp'.

At Larkhill we had three drill-orders on the ranges, very like those that we had had at Berkhamsted – but here, for the first time in our lives, we fired real shell. We still had only one gun per battery, so each battery in turn used all four guns belonging to the brigade.

Immediately after the conclusion of our firing practice, Withers and I were given four days leave. We knew that 'practice camp' was about the last stage in our training, and, though we were not told so definitely, we guessed that this would be our last leave before going overseas.

We rejoined the battery at Milford at the beginning of September. We heard that, during our absence, the division had been inspected by Lord Kitchener. That really did look like business!

During the ensuing week we received one day's training in trench warfare – all we ever had. The infantry having dug some trenches and ensconced themselves therein, the batteries took up positions behind. I was sent out in the middle of the night as 'forward observation officer'. I had only a very vague idea of my duties, for Keate had omitted (as usual) to give me any information or instructions. Nevertheless, I set out boldly on my white-legged chestnut, Prince, accompanied by Driver Lawlor on my second horse, a bay pony called Baby. I rode through a gap in our 'front line', and went and had a good look (as far as the darkness permitted) at a small square field some distance behind the enemy's line, which had been pointed out to me on the map as a possible target. I suppose that I was breaking the rules, but I did not feel that it mattered much, and I wanted to make sure that I had come to the right part of the line. Then Lawlor and I lay down beside our horses in a copse just behind our front line, and tried to sleep – not very successfully, for it was very cold – while parties of infantry crawled round us on their stomachs, presumably 'relieving'. About dawn I was recalled to the battery. Later, I went up to the top of a hill, whence I again perceived my field. And then we went home. Not an instructive affair!

2
THE FIRST BATTLE:
LOOS, 1915

I came to France in September 1915. Withers and I and the fifty-odd men who had come over on the *Empress Queen* arrived at Havre long before the rest of the battery. On arrival I formed the men up while Withers scouted around to find out what he was supposed to do with them. Eventually he returned with a small boy, who piloted us to another part of the docks and there left us to our own devices.

We sat down in the sun on the quay to wait. I wrote a long letter with a detailed, descriptive account of my wanderings so far, only to find when it was finished that I had written many things to which the censor would surely take exception. The men spent most of their time 'scrounging' round for water, but found none as every possible source of supply bore a neat inscription: 'For washing only – not to be drunk.' So ultimately we resigned ourselves to doing nothing, and sat still and watched the black-funnelled transports creeping in over the green water of the inner dock.

At last the *Inventor* appeared. All was scurry and confusion. Withers and I plunged into the bowels of the ship and began pushing unwilling horses up on slippery gangways. Keate dashed to and fro waving papers and waggling his chin – by the speed and nature of which operation it was possible for an acute observer to recognise the owner's temper.

We saw little of Havre. As soon as the whole battery was off the ship, we marched out to a rest camp, where we remained till midnight. In the early hours of the morning we returned to Havre and entrained.

The train left Havre about 4 a.m. We all slept until we had passed Rouen. We trundled along very slowly, by way of Abbeville and Boulogne, and passed through Calais at nightfall. We had started in ignorance of our destination, but had since been informed that we were bound for Audruicq, and on arriving there we proceeded to detrain. Before we had got far, a frantic Railway Transport Officer rushed up, put us all back in the train, and packed us off to St Omer.

At St Omer we detrained. Leaving the station about midnight, we set off to find the Calais road, but this proved too great a strain on Keate's powers of map-reading at that hour of the night, and we wandered several times round the town before we finally emerged into open country.

Our destination was the village of Tournehem, and there we arrived about dawn on the 13th. It was a dirty little village, and the officers lived in a dirty little 'pub', the Café Saniez Routier. Withers had gone forward from St Omer to find billets, but had contrived to miss the good ones set aside for us and to find nothing but our present humble lodgings.

At Tournehem we divided our time between grooming the horses and instructing the signallers, varied by occasional trips to the top of the hill behind the village whence we could hear the growling of the guns in Flanders. We did not realise that we were so far from the firing line, and gave ready credence to the rumours of impending action which circulated in the village.

On the 14th we all rode off to a field beside the Calais road, where the General Officer Commanding (GOC) for XI Corps addressed us. He told us that his corps, consisting of the 21st, 24th, and Guards Divisions, was being held in reserve, ready to keep the enemy on the move backwards as soon as the troops already facing him should have blown him out of his present trenches. His speech might have been quite inspiring, only that he did not appear to have noticed that he was addressing a gunner audience, and trotted out nothing but his stock infantry phrase about the platoon commander being the person to win the war.

Next day we marched away from Tournehem, and proceeded by way of Watteu – near which we turned into a field for the midday halt – to Staples, where we stayed for the night. Two colts greeted us with enthusiasm as we marched into the field which was to be our camp, and Withers roused the captain's ire by galloping after them on his horse and chasing them away.

In the morning Keate, Duncan, Sgt Lewis and a few gunners and signallers went off by bus to the 12th Divisional Artillery at Ploegsteert, to a battery of which they were attached for instruction for several days. Withers and I remained with the battery, which marched that day to St Jans Cappel.

St Jans was quite a pleasant place. Our horse lines were in a field on a hill above the village, and here the men bivouacked. The officers were billeted in a cottage close by.

Our chief difficulty was to obtain water for the horses. We solved the problem by damming a stream and so making a small reservoir, but a day or two later somebody dammed our stream higher up and cut off our water supply, so we had to water in the village.

At St Jans Cappel I took to myself a new horse, a bay pony called Bobby, from 'C' subsection. This minute horse had been a leader in the first team formed in the battery. He proved an excellent charger, and continued in that office for nearly two years.

From the neighbourhood of Croix de Poperinghe, just above our lines, we could obtain wide views over the sunlit plain of Flanders. The country stretched perfectly flat for miles, its details obscured by a faint haze, above which two rows of observation balloons, British and German, swung lazily at their cables. Hardly a sound broke the peace of this unnatural battleground.

It was at St Jans Cappel that we first paid the battery in francs – an incident small enough in itself, but deemed worthy of record in 134 separate pay-books.

We passed that night at La Miquellerie, near Busnes. As usual, the Battalion Quartermaster Sergeant (QMS) had gone ahead to find billets, and we were fixed up just as usual – men, horses and guns in a field, officers sleeping on the stone floor of a farmhouse room used also as a mess, and the captain on a bed in an adjoining room.

Next day a short march brought us to Bas Rieux, just outside Lillers. At first the brigade horse-lines were all together in one field – a broad, sunny expanse of green skirted by a stream – but, owing to fear of hostile aircraft, next morning we moved into smaller paddocks. Our lines occupied two orchards. I fear that, despite all our care, there was not as much fruit on those trees when we left as when we arrived.

It had now begun to rain, and for the first time the men we to be accommodated in barns. The thunder of the guns bey Bethune and Mazingarbe was continuous. At night the easte was alight with flashes and curving Very lights. In Flanders we had been struck with the silence of everything, but here even we realised that a heavy bombardment was in progress. We were not mistaken. For days the British and French guns had been bombarding the German lines stretched across Artois, preparing the way for the great offensive which was to carry us in triumph to the Rhine.

The March to Loos

At 3 p.m. on the 24th the officers of the 96th Brigade assembled at the farmhouse which served as Brigade HQ, and crowded into the office. Coates shut and locked the door, and, having made certain that he could not be overheard, spoke to this effect;

For many days our guns had been bombarding the enemy's trenches, which were now known to be 'completely pulverised' on all this part of the front. At dawn on the morrow the troops now in the line would advance against such of the enemy as had survived the bombardment, and would drive them out of their trenches. Once they were out and on the run, it was the business of XI Corps – our business – to keep them on the run, at least as far as the Rhine. No doubt could be entertained that the enemy's resistance would be completely broken: an even larger number of French troops would push northward from Champagne at the same moment as we pushed eastward from Artois. Caught in front and flank, the enemy could only run for it. We should leave our present camp that night, and move eastward. We should proceed by way of Vermelles and Hulluch to Pont à Vendin, where we were to bivouac on the night of the 25th/26th, and go on to Douai by the night of the 26th/27th. We must lighten our kits forthwith in order to be prepared for a long and rapid advance. Indeed the colonel's only fear was that the enemy might retreat so fast that we should be unable to get to blows with him.

Inspired, we all went off to tell our men all that it behoved them to know, and to pack things up ready for the 'long and rapid advance'. We left five green canvas armchairs and a stove belonging to the mess at Bas Rieux on leaving – stores which we never saw again. I have no doubt that madame sold them at great profit as soon as our backs were turned.

It was pouring with rain and very dark when we pulled out of our muddy orchard on to the road at about 10.30 p.m. that night, and set out for our first battlefield. We marched all night in the drenching rain, through silent shadowy villages, over crowded roads many inches deep in mire. We halted every few yards for varying periods – always just long enough for our saddles to get thoroughly wet. The heavy rain, borne on a biting wind, beat through our burberrys and drenched us to the skin. Our knees were wet, and the water trickled down our leggings and filled our boots. If we walked we were no better off, as the wet mud oozed in over our boot-tops. A few bits of chocolate which I had brought failed to cheer me. The long, slow march in the cold, driving rain would have been depressing indeed had we not been upheld by the knowledge that we were marching to victory, and that in a day or two all the world would ring with the fame of our achievement.

Dawn came at last. I had lost all count of the time long before the sky changed from a pitchy black to a very leaden grey. It still rained, and every forward step brought us onto a worse stretch of road. We were now following a river of red mud winding through a sodden countryside, which stretched out featureless into the fog on every hand.

At last, after a seemingly endless march, we turned up a track to the left, and ploughed up through the mud to a sodden windswept hilltop, rank with the smell of decaying cabbages. Here we bivouacked. Our servants spread our valises under waterproof sheets between four gaunt haystacks which loomed up dark and dismal on the hilltop, but it was broad day before we got 'down to it', as we had to take the horses a long way to water and see that they were fed before making ourselves comfortable.

After a few hours we awoke. The rain had ceased and the sun shone palely through a wet fog. On a road below us we could see cavalry and horse artillery moving up at a trot towards the battlefield.

I had just finished shaving – using the back of the mess-cart as my table – and was making ready to enjoy my breakfast, when a panting orderly rushed up with orders to move at once. We had just time to gulp down a gingerbread biscuit each and a cup of tea – shared between four – while the teams were hooking in. Then off we went again.

Very soon after we started it began to rain again. Wet and hungry as we were when we started on the day's march, it was even worse than that of the night before. The rain came down steadily: we were soon wet through again, and we got gradually colder and colder. Nor could we keep ourselves warm by walking, as the mud flowed into our boots and passing vehicles drenched us with liquid ooze. Further, our stomachs grew emptier and emptier with each hour that passed, and every moment we became more sleepy.

The road was packed with traffic of all kinds. Artillery, engineers, ambulances – horsed and motor – infantry transport and lorries struggled for room in the strip of red mud which was called a road. Under these circumstances it was a matter of the greatest difficulty, demanding constant vigilance, to keep in touch with the people in front, and to avoid getting lost.

We had no maps, and the sodden grey landscape, utterly featureless, over which we passed, gave us no clue to our whereabouts. We were caught up and whirled on, or cast aside and left stranded on the edge of a vast stream of traffic, flowing ever eastwards. Halts were even more frequent than during the night. Occasionally we passed a miserable house by the wayside, from the doorstep of which sodden, unwashed children gazed at us in wonder. But we could not see far. All but the nearest objects were shut off from our view by a screen of driving rain.

Far on in the afternoon we entered Noeux-les-Mines, having traversed at most 1 mile per hour during the day. The press of vehicles was slightly less in the town, and we were able to look about us. We squelched on along roads inches deep in black mud, past steaming slag-heaps and grimy houses. Faces, wet, dirty and dishevelled, gazed at us from filthy pavements and soot-encrusted windows. Numbers of walking wounded were passing through – the less severely damaged of the warriors of the 9th and 15th Divisions trickling back from the battlefield. All seemed cheerful and wished us Godspeed. So we passed on out of the town, ready for whatever might befall.

Darkness fell as we drew out of the town. We turned off the road and unhooked the teams beside a railway embankment. Withers and I spent over an hour in watering the horses: there was great competition for a leaky canvas trough, fed by a pump which worked by fits and starts. Just as we got back, conscious of work well done and eager for tea, Keate met us with orders to hook in again and go on at once.

At about 8 p.m., then, we set off again, back on the same old road, still trekking eastwards. There seemed little hope of reaching Pont-à-Verdin that night, though, for all I knew, we might have been just entering it even then.

As a matter of fact, we were just approaching Mazingarbe. The road was now black and slippery, instead of red and sticky as heretofore. Halts were frequent: on one occasion we stopped beside quite a large body of German prisoners – the first we had seen.

We clattered through darkened Mazingarbe. All around us our heavies were thundering: we had reached the front. Dazed by the noise, we moved on in a stream of transport, all bound towards the battlefield.

Suddenly we halted. The order came down: 'Reverse the Vehicles.' Before we had decided how to carry out this difficult operation on a road where wagons were jammed wheel to wheel, a second order came down, cancelling the first. I went up to the head of the column and found Withers, who had led us so far, but now had lost all touch with the rest of the brigade, and was very uncertain of his whereabouts.

We waited for some time. Then the colonel appeared, and, spitting and swearing vehemently, led us along a road to the right, the main Bethune–Lens road. It transpired afterwards that we were the only battery in the brigade which had fetched up at the appointed place – the crossroads at Philosophe. The others were straying all over the countryside, but were eventually collected behind us at 'Victoria Station'.

Here we stood then, on the Lens road – how far from the enemy we knew not. The time was about midnight on 25/26 September and we were the leading battery of the 21st Division. The rain had stopped, but it would have been very dark except for the flashes of the guns all round us. The noise was deafening. To the right, in front and to the left the Very lights rose and fell, making it appear as though we were almost surrounded. Now and then a small party of infantry would dart between the wagons, cross the road and vanish into the gloom of the Rutoire plain. Too tired even to be excited, we leant against the wagons and slept.

The Battle
We stood there on the wet road for some time. Finally the captain appeared – where he had been I do not know – and led us up a road to the right, bringing us into action in a field. There was no galloping about: we just came up in column of route, and each gun unlimbered independently in the place appointed. We immediately set to and dug pits about 2 feet deep into which we ran the guns. Each gun had its wagon beside it. No slit trenches were dug till later. We continued digging till dawn. The moon shone now and, combined with the enemy's innumerable Very lights, gave us so bright a light that discovery seemed inevitable. I had no idea how far we were from the enemy. By dawn we had finished digging and the men had breakfast. Duncan had

selected a position for the wagon-line and had then retired to bed, preparatory to assuming the details of observation officer on Fosse 7 at dawn. The rest of us retired to bed in a deserted house in 'Quality Street' about 9 a.m. Meanwhile the other batteries of the brigade, and later the other brigades, had also come into action. At dawn the 96th Brigade Ammunition Column found itself just outside Loos village, and our wagon-line was found also to be in front of our gun-position. Both were moved back, the wagon-line to a sheltered position behind the fosse at Les Brebis, and the column to Mazingarbe.

I awoke at noon to find Keate and Withers gone. I shaved, breakfasted and went out. Keate was prowling up and down at the gun-position, stroking his chin. It appeared that reports of a severe reverse had been received, and that, at any moment, our infantry, hotly pursued by the enemy, might retire through the guns. The captain seemed also to believe that a large gas cloud was approaching, which might at any moment envelop and overwhelm us. Keate then retired to rest, leaving me in charge at the guns. I had the 'wind right up', but as the sun shone and nothing untoward happened, I speedily came back to my original idea that, at most, the check was very slight and that at any moment the advance might be resumed. Fortified by this conclusion, I sat down with my feet in a wire-trench behind the guns and wrote a letter. The day was fine and fairly quiet. We were in action on a forward slope, with 'D' battery close behind. In front were four 60-pounders in whose neighbourhood occasional 'crumps' burst – the first German shells I saw.

That night I slept under a trolley on the gun-position. The colonel rang up to tell us to be ready to move forward at any moment, but, as a matter of fact, the night passed quietly. My rest was disturbed only by an occasional trolley-load of wounded passing rearwards along the track which ran through the position. Next morning I went up on to the fosse, but the mist was very thick, and I could see nothing. After a while Walters – my servant – brought me up a cold breakfast of fried bacon and tea, and then the sergeant major came along, armed with orders and a map. It appeared that I was to go forward to a position on a hill above Loos, whence I could better observe the movements of our infantry. I was to take two men to dig me a hole to sit in, and the sergeant major would follow with telephonists. The day before, Withers had been sent forward with Bombardier Cantwell to establish touch with the 64th Brigade, but had run into a cloud of gas, and had returned slightly gassed, the richer by one mule. Aware of this, I set out with some trepidation.

I was not allowed to take the map – there was only one in the battery and that had nothing on it – so I should certainly have been lost had I not met Conolly of 'B' battery on the Lens road, bent on the same quest. So he and I, with his telephonists and my grave-diggers – a cheerful reminder these, most considerately provided by Keate – set out together. We turned to the left off the Lens road, crossed our old front line, passed through the torn fragments of the enemy's wire entanglements, and arrived at the trench which had been his front line till our attack two days before. Damaged it was, and blown in here and there, but hardly 'pulverised', as we had been told. Here and there a young German lay on his face in the bottom of the trench, half trampled into the mud, and already serving as food for rats and insects.

We passed on. The whole air was tainted with the odour of chlorine gas, mingled with those of dead bodies and HEs. Here and there horses and fragments of vehicles lay on the grass. Behind a tumbling haystack I found Vyvyan of D/95 and gave him a drink out of my water bottle. Further on we saw another stack. One by one we sprinted to it across the grass, and, safe behind it, took up our abode in a large shell-hole. After a while Battery Sergeant Major S. M. Walker appeared with a string of telephonists – enough to give any Observation Post (OP) away.

33

Under his direction they started to lay a line back to the battery. By this time 5.9-inch shells were falling round about. One caught Gunner McAllister – one of the telephonists – on head and ankle, and the sergeant major, picking him up, carried him under shell-fire to the safety of the nearest trench. During the day my telephonists laid three lines to the battery and Conolly's one, but neither of us ever succeeded in obtaining communication. We had only the new No. 25 enamelled wire, which was cut as soon as it was laid down.

We remained in our hole all the morning. The rotting haystack which gave us cover stood on the top of a hill facing Hill 70. The Bois Hugo, Bois Rase and Puits 14 bis were immediately in front. The Ferme des Mines de Lens, Douvrin church and the Metallurgique de Wingles were also visible – we used the last two to re-sect our position. Loos village and our positions in the valley below us were hidden by the curve of the hill. We stayed where we were all day. The morning was sunny and fairly quiet. An occasional aeroplane or a few greenish bursts of chlorine shell alone interrupted the blue vaults of the sky. Now and then a bunch of crumps fell near us, and shells burst continually over the Lens–Bethune road behind us. In the afternoon a heavy bombardment began, the guns banging away behind us and the white bursts of 18-pounder shrapnel obscuring the green slope of Hill 70. The shells seemed to be passing just over our heads, and nothing would have induced me to get out of the hole and stand upright on the ground. But Conolly chose this moment to leave me and crawl round on his stomach to see if he could find King of 'A' battery, whom he believed to be in some not very distant trench. The enemy made scant reply to our fire. A few shrapnel burst high overhead and one jagged piece passed through a gunner's coat, which was lying on the side of our hole.

At 5 p.m. the bombardment ceased and the Guards attacked. We could see them going on up the hill at a walk – on and on, despite the gaps made in their ranks by the fire of the enemy's machine-guns from the edge of the Bois Hugo. Before they gained the edge of the wood, twilight settled down over the valley and they were lost to sight. This being so, we decided to go home. Many people were now strolling about our hill, chatting and smoking, apparently discussing the day's battle as calmly as though it had been a cricket match, just concluded in the calm of a summer's evening – all undisturbed by the enemy. We therefore took courage to emerge from our hole, and went off as fast as we could towards Fosse 7. On the way we walked indiscreetly close in front of an 18-pounder and narrowly escaped destruction. When we arrived, we found that the batteries had moved. Conolly found 'B' battery just at the foot of the fosse, but I wandered for hours over the starlit plain – covered with long grass and strewn with coils of loose wire – before I found 'C'. On hearing that I belonged to the 21st Division, the passers-by of whom I sought direction would have nothing to do with me. [This was because the 21st Division was thought by the men of the Regular Army not to have pulled their weight].

I got home very late and went to sleep on the floor of our new mess, a house in Maroc. Next day Withers went out as FOO, but he was recalled about 9 a.m., and, accompanied by Bombardier Priestley and guided by a signaller of 'D' battery, I went out to find their OP. The state of the battlefield was even less inviting than on the previous day, none of the dead having yet been buried. The smell of gas was less pronounced and that of decaying flesh more so. I found Timson of D/96 and Colliser of B/97 together at the entrance of a deep dug-out in the old German trenches. The dug-out lay under many feet of earth and was lined with concrete. In the bottom the telephonists of the two batteries reclined on mouldy straw.

It was understood that, as the Guards had failed to take Hill 70 on the previous day, a fresh attack was to be made. I sent Priestley forward, as ordered, to get into touch with the Commanding Officer of the 2nd Scots Guards. Passing through Loos village, he discharged his mission, but lost himself on the way back, and finally arrived at the battery long after dark. No attack took place, and towards the end of the afternoon Keate recalled me to the guns. I went back with one of 'D' battery's telephonists. Crossing the old No Man's Land, we passed among the bodies of many Highlanders, who lay on their faces, row on row, facing the enemy's positions, where they had fallen in the first attack. After that we did no forward observation. Keate observed all day from the concrete water-tower at Maroc, relieved occasionally by Withers, me, or the sergeant major. Coates was acting as CRA, and Duncan was away acting as his *aide-de-camp*, the brigade being temporarily commanded by Major McGowan of 'D' battery.

Withers and I shared duty at the guns, one of us sleeping each night in a little grave dug in the chalk and roofed with an old door. An adjoining chamber sheltered the telephonists. The guns were sunk about two feet into the ground, with their wagons beside them, as in the first position – in three cases the wagon limber and the body were one on either side of the gun, but this arrangement was condemned by the colonel as offering a wider target. Attached to each pit was a frail dug-out, roofed only with an old door or two, for the gunners. The officers and sergeants messed in houses in Maroc – deserted, of course, but containing a certain amount of furniture, and very little damaged considering how close they were to the old front line.

Several days passed peacefully. I have a vivid recollection, one sunny day, of sitting undisturbed on the position censoring letters, while enemy shells burst over the Lens road on our left. The nights were quiet, too – except that the sentry used to complain of being sniped whenever he moved, and Nash rang up at 1 a.m. every morning to query the ammunition return of the night before. One night eight guns – all that was left of the 94th Brigade after their 'doing' on the 26th – came up into action behind us. On another occasion Withers tried to lay out the night lines on a star – a perfectly sound method – to the great amusement of the Nos 1. At 7 p.m. on 1 October I was sent to a point on the Lens–Bethune road to meet part of a battery which was relieving us. I had only just heard that we were to be relieved, and had no idea what battery I was to meet. Withers joined me and we waited until 11 p.m., when A/63 rolled up. As this appeared to be the battery we wanted, we laid hold of them and took them up to our position.

The right section withdrew to the wagon-line under Withers, while Keate and I stayed on at Maroc. The next morning was fine, and a hostile aeroplane flew over the positions. His visit soon bore fruit. During the early part of the afternoon an 8-inch howitzer shelled 'D' battery. Only a few shots fell on the position, but 2nd-Lt O' Neil was wounded in the knee. He had been commanding during McGowan's absence at HQ. At 1.20 p.m. the sergeant major, Sgt McGowan and I were sunning ourselves behind a wagon, and an 8-inch shell landed within 4 yards of us, covering us with dirt but miraculously harming none of us. When we had collected our senses, we withdrew the detachments from our two guns which, with the telephone dug-out were heavily shelled. A/63's guns were not shelled, and Sitwell and his men remained in their pits. As we were not firing at the time I did not consider that I should be justified in keeping the men in the danger area, and my decision to withdraw them was supported by Keate.

The enemy fired twenty-four rounds, causing some damage to our emplacements. Bombardier Russell and the sergeant major remained in the telephone dug-out throughout. As soon as the firing ceased we returned to the guns and stayed there all the rest of the long afternoon, being relieved after dusk by the remaining section of A/63. On relief we withdrew to the wagon-line, where we slept. Withers and I spent the night in a cold dug-out in company with a bombardier – I don't know who. Rising early we partook of a cold breakfast – Keate sulking throughout – and, getting to horse about 10 a.m., moved off by way of Mazingarbe to a plain outside Noeux-les-Mines, there to camp for the night. And so ended my first battle.

3
TRENCH WARFARE, 1915-1916

The Downfall of Keale

Bit by bit, from what we heard afterwards, we were able to piece together some history of the Battle of Loos. Before we left Maroc we had realised, of course, that the expected breakthrough had not occurred, but why we did not know, though we understood that the 21st Division had failed to accomplish what was expected of it and, not to put too fine a point on it, that the infantry had run away. The facts were these. The attack was delivered by the following divisions in this order, from right to left: 47th, 15th, 1st, 7th, 9th, 2nd. The 47th (London Territorial Force) Division fought hard and succeeded in making a limited advance despite the enemy's resistance at the 'Double Crassier', a formidable obstacle. The 2nd Division, on the left, astride the La Basseé Canal, failed to advance at all, owing to neglect to cut the enemy's wire, thus narrowing the front on which success was possible and diminishing our chance of victory. The four divisions in the centre of the attack, breaking through the enemy's front-line defences, already partially reduced by our artillery fire, pressed on further and further into the enemy's country. Owing (presumably) to bad management on the part of the staff, the attacking troops became involved with our own gas cloud, which had preceded the attack. Such as survived this pressed right on, either because the staff had omitted to limit their objectives or because, having orders, the troops themselves failed to obey them. At any rate our troops, devoid of all cohesion, were caught as scattered elements by the enemy's counter-attack and were everywhere driven back.

Meanwhile the XI Corps – the 21st, 24th and Guards Divisions – had arrived upon the scene. They had marched for some thirty hours through the rain and were tired, hungry, wet and depressed. The staffs concerned had neglected to provide adequate traffic control with the result that these divisions, having to jostle their way through crowds of transport, arrived late upon the field. Further, the staff had failed to ensure the arrival of their rations, to give them rest after their tiring march before throwing them into the fight, or to provide them with maps and information. I think I am right in saying that all the infantry of the 21st Division had to go on were some little pencil sketches of one or two prominent landmarks, made by an officer of the divisional staff.

Whether the higher staffs knew where the enemy was when the 21st Division came up, I do not know. If so, they neglected to pass on the information to the troops. The result was that the infantry of the division, believing the enemy to be still far to the east of Hill 70, came on in column of fours, tired and hungry, over the crest where our front line had been, and were greeted by the enemy – who had in fact regained possession of Hill 70 – with concentrated machine gun fire, from which they suffered heavily. The infantry of the division remained in the line one night. They had nothing to eat – the divisional train was caught and destroyed by the enemy's guns on the Bethune–Lens road, and its wrecked vehicles filed along the roadside were reproduced in photographs as 'wrecked German transport'. The division – under fire for the first time – lost an appreciable portion of the ground it had been ordered to hold, suffered 8,000 casualties, and on the evening of the 26th its shattered remnants were withdrawn.

It cannot be denied that, even under the circumstances, the 21st Division might have done better. The 24th Division did no better. In comparing the achievements of these divisions with those of the Guards Division, it must be remembered that the former were thrown into battle immediately after a trying march, hungry, worn-out, wet through and without information as to the whereabouts of the enemy, while the latter – I believe – had at least one day's rest and did not come into action until the staffs concerned had had time to inform themselves in regard to the situation. Further, while the Guards had fought in France since the beginning of the war, and were fortified both by experience and by traditions, the 21st and 24th Divisions were fresh from England, and had never seen a shot fired: nor had they received any training in warfare of quite this character.

Meanwhile the artillery of the 21st Division, though despised and rejected by General Wardrop, who commanded the Guards Division artillery – a poor show – had, by general consent, acquitted themselves pretty well. The 96th Brigade was the first on the scene, being in action south of the Lens road by dawn. The 94th and 85th Brigades came into action above Loos, the former on a forward slope, while their wagon-lines moved about the Rutoire plain. The 94th was in large measure destroyed by the enemy's guns and withdrew, the remnant of it coming into action at Maroc later on.

Throughout the battle, Coates had been in command of the divisional artillery. General Alexander was sent home and at Hondeghem Brigadier General R. A. C. Wellesley joined us and took command, Coates returning to the brigade. General Forrestier, GOC Division, and a number of other officers were also sent home, our new divisional commander being major General C. R. Jacob. We expected a long rest at Hondeghem, but on the day after our arrival we were told to hold ourselves in readiness to move, and next day Keate, Duncan, I and the left section set out by way of 'Les Trois Peupliers', Bailleul and Nieppe to Armentières.

All this time Keate had been at war with Withers. First of all, the Staples incident had annoyed him. Then Withers' failure to come to our assistance on 2 October had incensed him, and finally he had found one or two rugs off in Withers' section – before 'Rug-Up' but, still – at Noeux-les-Mines. There had been war to the knife and, though the colonel had patched up a peace at Hondeghem, we all realised that fighting might break out afresh almost at any moment.

We found the 50th (Northumbrian) Division in possession at Armentières. We spent the afternoon under the trees beside the canal, and, after dark, we pulled our two guns into two of the pits vacated by the 3rd Battery, 1st Northumbrian Brigade (Territorial Force), their guns remaining in action in the other two pits. The battery was commanded by a Major Johnson, who remained until his other section was relieved, to show us round. A subaltern of his took me down to the trenches, which struck me as palatial places after the Loos trenches, and gave me an exhibition of ranging. He was attempting to range one of my guns on the enemy's front line and, though he did not observe a single round, he kept on giving such directions as 'Plus, I think – drop 100' or 'I think plus and to the right – 30 more left, drop 50'. After firing about a score of rounds and dropping some 400 yards, having seen no shots at all, he concluded this remarkable display of 'close-shooting' – the enemy's trench being about 200 yards from our own.

The battery kept an officer always in the trenches. This officer observed all day, and at night slept at battalion HQ, where he also took his meals, except lunch. He was known as the FOO or Forward Observing Officer. I went down as FOO on the 8th and my tour was supposed to last for forty-eight hours, but Duncan relieved on the 9th. That evening the right section came in. Withers' horse had fallen with him outside Bailleul and had crushed his ankle, so he had had to ride the rest of the way on a wagon. Withers' helplessness infuriated Keate, who was further angered by the absence of Sgt Lewis, who had had a similar accident at Hondeghem the day before – after Keate had come up to Armentières. He appeared to hold Withers personally to blame for both accidents. Hard words passed and next day the useless Withers was packed off in the cook's cart (with his hat at his feet and an expression of injured innocence on his face) to the Brigade Ammunition Column at Nieppe. 2nd-Lt J. S. Stower, who had been with the battery in England, was to join us in his stead.

That morning I woke up in a particularly bad temper – it was 10 October – and took the opportunity to sack my servant – a long-contemplated move. I sent Driver Walters off to the wagon-line. But the chief excitement of that day was yet to come. In the evening Melle came round and ordered Keate to 'register' the enemy's front line opposite Trench 74 – slightly to the left of the trench which we had by this time registered successfully. He sent me off to measure off the ranges and angles from the map, but before I had completed my task I heard the guns fire eight rounds in quick succession. Coming down a moment later with the measured ranges, I found Keate striding up and down outside the telephone dug-out, stroking his chin. In great agitation he informed me that he had fired into our own trenches and had killed four men and wounded several others in our front line. Duncan was promptly recalled from the trenches, and I was sent down. Needless to say, the infantry did not welcome me with effusion. After two days I returned to the battery for the Court of Inquiry into the incident, which was held at No. 96, Rue Victor Hugo, on 14 October.

The Court was composed of officers whom I did not know. Coates, Keate, Duncan, I and two infantry officers attended as witnesses. Duncan and I unfortunately left our hats in the court room, so I had to give my evidence in Melle's – a large floppy one, which kept on slipping right down over my nose. Completing my evidence, I seized up the two hats from the window-sill and made off.

That night Keate was in the mess and the colonel rang him up. I was in the telephone dug-out trying to get on to someone else and an imperfect switchboard enabled me to hear most of what passed. Keate was suspended from command from that moment, and I was to be Officer Commanding battery until the following morning, when Captain G. L. Johnstone of the column would arrive to take command. When I went into the mess, Keate told me of this, and for some fifteen hours I was in command of the battery. At the end of that time – 9 a.m. on 15 October – Johnstone arrived and Keate duly handed over to him and withdrew to head-quarters. There he remained until 4 November. I met him now and then and he was always affable – once I remember in Trench 73 Support where he was wandering round in slacks and shoes. Finally he went to England, and there received command of a battery of the 39th Division, then training at Milford. What happened to him after that I do not know – two years later I noticed his name in the *Gazette*, to be major while acting as second in command of a prisoners of war camp.

And that was the last we saw of Keate. The battery was overjoyed to see the last of him, for the men hated him and not without cause – one of the things which most roused their resentment being his habit of making all the gunners walk all the way when the battery was on the march. We all turned with enthusiasm to the service of Capt. Johnstone.

Raids and Bombardments

The day of Dalton's arrival was marked by a mishap. Certain gunners were loading a wagon when a shell struck a house above them and splinters wounded three of them – Fillingham, Damme and Sherwood. Two were seriously wounded, and all were taken to hospital. Just at this time, as D/97 had left the division and the other howitzer batteries were attached each to one 18-pounder brigade, Lt-Col Pottinger, Officer Commanding (OC) 97th Brigade, found himself without a tactical command. He therefore took part of the CPO – Central Plotting Office, i.e. the local 'flash-spotters' – and moved his household from No. 96 Rue Victor Hugo to the centre of the town: and Dalton, dissatisfied with our existing mess, took possession of No. 96.

That part of the town which lay between us and the asylum was almost deserted and had been much battered by shellfire. One day some 50 yards of house-wall fell down for no apparent reason, exposing the battered interiors of several deserted dwellings. Few houses in this part of the town boasted complete roofs, and such persons as continued to live in this quarter – from which the country behind the enemy's lines was clearly visible – laid themselves open naturally to the suspicion of being spies. We had one or two spy-hunts among the deserted half-mined houses, but found nothing. On one occasion, however, our guard arrested two high officers of the divisional staff, and dragged them before Dalton at about one o'clock in the morning. There was nothing for it, of course, but to apologise, give them drinks and let them go, and this Dalton did, coming down in gum-boots and pyjamas.

Meanwhile the division was growing steadily in efficiency. The 50th Division, apparently, had worked on the formation of letting sleeping dogs lie, and when we arrived the sector was the quietest on the British front. But we conceived it to be our duty always to harass the Bosch; and to do everything in our power to cause him casualties. We were told that the surest to end the war was to kill Germans, and this we set about doing, with the result that we quickly changed this part of the front from the sleepiest to one of the liveliest sectors that I have seen.

Each side shelled the trenches of the other, and the town was heavily bombarded by the enemy. In reply to our bombardment on 8 December he fired some hundreds of shells into Armentières. On the whole remarkably little damage was done, though Dalton found his way up from the wagon-line blocked by burning houses. One of our hens became a casualty but otherwise we were unharmed.

Our 'stunts' and the enemy's retaliation made us less and less popular with the citizens of Armentières. We had already fired an organised shoot on Fort Sennarmount, and proposed to bombard something or other on the 11th, but our large expenditure of ammunition in reply to the enemy's shelling of the town on the 8th and 9th prevented it.

But the biggest show of all was to come off on the 15th, and all its details were openly discussed all over the town weeks beforehand. After a long preparatory bombardment, 100 men of the 8th Somersets were to sally forth from the 'mushroom' – an excrescence of ill repute, protruding in front of Trench 70 – enter the enemy's lines, and bring back alive as many Huns as possible as prisoners. The raid thus undertaken was, I believe, the first ever undertaken by British, other than Canadian troops.

The 15th duly arrived. I laid a wire to Trench 71 Support and attempted to direct our fire from there. In view of the fact that our 9.2-inch and 12-inch howitzers were bombarding the 'Railway Salient', a portion of the enemy's trench projecting to within about 150 yards of our Trench 72, the infantry holding Trenches 71 and 72 were withdrawn to the support line. The enemy seemed aware of this and shelled Trench 71 Support heavily for some hours with guns and howitzers of all calibres up to 5.9-

inch, overturning the sandbag breastworks and causing many casualties. A 5.9 shell actually landed on the traverse beside which I crouched, but buried itself without bursting in the soft mud.

The bombardment consisted of three spasms. After the first, unable to keep my new wire intact, I adjourned to my usual OP in Bay 17 (Trench 72), accompanied by Bombardier Kettle, and observed from there. I was immediately in front of our new telephone dug-out, which the enemy apparently mistook for a trench-mortar emplacement and shelled vigorously. Also our own 12-inch shells burst sometimes as little as 50 yards in front, and an occasional round of 18-pounder shrapnel burst over or even behind our trench. So my position was far from comfortable, but the wire held and I was able to control the fire of the battery. Further, my presence was a great comfort to the two luckless sentries who had been left in the trench in case of emergency. The presence of a gunner officer with them in a 'strafe' always gives the infantry great pleasure and increased confidence, and they always welcome him warmly – or nearly always.

All at once the battery stopped firing. It appeared that a hostile 4.2-inch howitzer, in action south-west of Perenchies had fired five rounds on to the position – no uncommon occurrence – and that one of these rounds had fallen on No. 1 gun-pit, smashing through the frail roof and bursting over the breech of the gun. Of the detachment, Sgt McGowan and two men were severely wounded and the other three men were killed.

That night Bombardier Radcliffe and five gunners joined us as reinforcements. The gun was little damaged, but we fired our 'box barrage' with only three guns. The actual raid occurred at 3.25 a.m. on 16 December. It was preceded by three minutes' bombardment of the point to be raided, and the raiders at work were enclosed in a 'box barrage'. Many of the enemy were slain and seven prisoners taken. Two officers had been caught in their pyjamas: one died fighting in the trench, and the other – according to report – steadfastly refusing to walk across No Man's Land till he put his boots on, was shot.

Withers had relieved me in Trench 72, and Denvir was acting as 'Liaison Officer' with the Somersets in Trench 70. Next morning I went off to the cemetery of St Jean le Bon for the funeral of the three gunners, but this did not actually take place till the afternoon. By that time Coates had rung up and ordered us to be out of action by 5 p.m., and to proceed to La Menegate, near Steenverek, for a rest.

We pulled out soon after the appointed time, but, owing to a hitch which had occurred in the matter of ammunition, we had to make a long halt in Pont de Nieppe, and did not reach La Menegate till very late. With us we brought a goose, secured by arrangement from Mr Ireland's pen, and, though it had one or two falls from the General Service (GS) wagon on the way, it tasted excellent on Christmas Day.

We were out for ten days. After five days at La Menegate we moved to Noote Boom, near Bailleul. It had rained incessantly for some two months, and was still raining. A stream in front of the farm where we lodged continued to rise, until on Christmas Eve the road and farmyard were flooded. Next day, however, the water fell slightly.

We had a very cheery Christmas, the men having an excellent dinner of pork, plum pudding and beer, followed by football and a concert. Their letters home were full of gratitude to us, particularly the captain, whom one of them described as 'a prince to the one we came out with'.

While we were out at rest, Sgt Goacher – one of the Nos 1 and the inventor of an ingenious 'flash-spotter' – left us, and went home to make munitions. I took his grey horse Mick as my charger. Sgt Jones became No. 1 of 'D' subsection, and Cpl Brooks promoted to sergeant of 'C' subsection. I would have preferred to promote Cpl Priestley, but Dalton thought him too young. Cpl Porter, the NCO in charge of the signallers, became sergeant.

Of officers, there now remained only Dalton, Denvir and myself. Duncan had gone home on 7 December to make munitions, and Withers, who had rejoined us in his place, had gone back to the column when we came out of action.

Going back into action on 26 December, we marched along flooded roads and, on arriving at the position, had the misfortune to get one of the guns off the track, sunk in the mud above the axle. Though we arrived on the position at nightfall, we did not get that gun into action till 2 a.m.

It rained all that night and the gun-pits quickly became flooded. In view of this, and the proved inadequacy of our present cover, we set about constructing new pits, made with 'elephant' cupolas covered with sandbags with broken bricks. The telephone pit was also flooded out, and we built a new one in a broken-down hut on the left flank of the battery. The orderly officer slept in an adjacent house, his old dug-out having long ago been flooded – one morning Denvir woke to find about a foot of water on the floor.

We thought that our cupolas could keep anything out, but one day, while No. 1 gun-pit was in course of reconstruction, the enemy put a 'whizz-bang' through the top. HQ asked for a full description of the damage done and Sgt Porter furnished them with nine explanatory drawings, and I with one. Somewhat disappointed in our cupolas, we finished off the gun-pits, and then started on the men's dug-outs. Unfortunately, owing to the flooded state of the ground, we were unable to dig down, and both gun-pits and dug-outs stood about 10 feet high from the ground, and absolutely invited bombardment.

By this time leave had started. Dalton was away from 1–10 January, and our old friend Johnstone came up from the column to take command. Denvir was sick, and I was the only officer available for trench duty – we now covered the Lincolns and Middlesex in trenches 68 and 69 – so Johnstone did a spell down there. He came down to relieve me on the 3rd, when a German 8-inch howitzer was throwing shells over us at B/94's position in Chapelle d'Armentières.

On the 5th we received a new officer in the person of 2nd-Lt O Murray Lyon, who came from the Divisional Artillery Column (DAC), but had previously been with me in the 95th Brigade. I went to tea at Brigade HQ and met him, and then went on to Col Pottinger's new HQ – the two brigades lived near one another in the Rue Sadi Carnot. It appeared that the caretaker at No. 96 Rue Victor Hugo had complained that, between us, Pottinger and we had broken open the bathroom door and stolen some crockery and a large doll. While I admitted breaking open the door, and it was well known that he had the crockery, no one would confess to having carried the '*grande poupee*'.

Dalton returned about the 10th, and Johnstone went back to the column. We still saw him pretty often, as the officer who visited the wagon-line was in the habit of lunching at the column on at least one out of his two days. At this time Johnstone, Botting, Withers – except when he was with us – and Stower, who afterwards went to Trench Mortars, were with the column, and they had all at different times been with 'C' battery.

On 11 January the enemy's 8-inch howitzer shelled D/96, who were in action in front of the asylum, but most of the shells fell well short and no damage was done. We believed the enemy could hear our telephone conversations, as we had only earth circuits and earth-pins in our front line, and, in view of this, Major McGowan repeatedly told his FOO in the trenches that the enemy's shells were falling 'right on the position' in the hope that, overhearing this, they would not alter their range, and would continue to fire short. Whether the Hun overheard and, if so, whether he took account of these messages, we did not know: at any rate he did not increase his range.

I foresaw that the 8-inch howitzer, which was believed to be at Lomme, would attack us – the next battery on the left – on the 19th, and we made arrangements to withdraw the men to the mess cellars. Sure enough, at a quarter to nine on the day appointed, a terrific explosion shook the mess, and I rushed out just in time to see the second shell close to No. 3 gun. I rang up Dalton, who was not yet down, and received orders to withdraw the men. Some of them showed a remarkable disinclination to take cover, as they were in the middle of shaving etc. for the 9 a.m. parade. When I had got them all off the position, and had directed them to the cellars beneath the mess, I returned to the telephone dug-out and arranged with 'B' and 'D' Batteries to cover zone during the morning, and then came away with the telephonists. By this time shells of several calibres were falling on the position, usually around Nos 3 and 4 gun-pits and the telephone dug-out, and two aeroplanes could be seen ranging the enemy's howitzers on to our pits. One of these was brought down by our anti-aircraft guns, but the other accomplished his task before going home.

We all spent the morning in the cellar. The sergeants were supposed to remain in their mess, but, as a matter of fact, Sgt Mackrill stood about at the 'octroi' controlling the traffic – a job for which he was well qualified being a policeman by profession – and Sgt Jones went around the gun-position under fire and brought in the dial-sights of the guns, which had been forgotten. I went round with him on his last trip, when we removed the sight from No. 1 gun. A dead Frenchman lay in a shop near the 'octroi'. The 'octroi' itself had been almost demolished, and the road round it and all the ground between that and No. 4 gun-pit had been torn up by the heavy shells. A shell must have burst just at the entrance to No. 4 pit, for the cupola had been riddled with splinters and the gun, with its carriage bent and broken, lay wheel-less on a bed of cinders. Only one shell landed on the position while we were there, an 8-inch, which roared over us and burst some 10 yards beyond. For bringing in these sights under fire Sgt Jones received the Distinguished Conduct Medal.

I spent the afternoon on the wagon-line. On returning to the battery at dusk, I found that the enemy's fire had ceased. Expecting him to shell the position with smaller guns during the night, Dalton kept the men in the cellars. Denvir and I walked round the position, over which brooded a strange silence and a strong smell of HE. The shells, forming craters 4 yards wide and as many feet deep, had unearthed all sorts of bones and sheep's skulls from beneath the soil of the market garden in which the pits stood. Coming to the pits, we found that Nos 2 and 3 had been crushed in on the guns, the former receiving three and the latter two direct hits. No. 1 pit, the most exposed of all, alone remained untouched.

The enemy had paid us the compliment of expending some 400 shells, at a low estimate, to encompass our destruction, and not less than 100 of these had been of 8-inch calibre. We were probably justified in congratulating ourselves on having caused him some damage!

That evening Murray Lyon was recalled from the trenches, and it was decided that we should withdraw to our wagon-line. The shattered guns were accordingly extricated from the ruins by Sgt Jones during the next afternoon, and the limbers came up to remove them. During the day the divisional commander, with the CRA of the division and those of the Corps and of the flank divisions, as well as many other officers, came to have a look round our pits. The 'elephant' pit was a comparatively new thing, and ours were probably the first to suffer extinction, so that some instruction was to be gained from a tour of them.

Our departure in the evening was somewhat hastened by the fact that a suspicious-looking woman, after hanging round for some time, was reported by a passing 'padre' to have vanished into a tall house facing the enemy's lines. We marched down to Pont-de-Nieppe, and next day I took the three damaged guns to the Army Ordnance Department workshops at Bailleul. Their battered condition attracted many curious eyes en route. A few days later three new guns were drawn from Steenwerck railhead.

A Subaltern's Week

The kind of warfare in which we were now engaged was so monotonous that it was possible to arrange a regular programme of officers' duties. Withers came and went so uncertainly that, though he was some years my senior, the duties of senior subaltern devolved upon me, and I was responsible for the allotment of duties, etc. It was ordained by the higher authorities that an officer's tour of duty as FOO should be forty-eight hours, and so we arranged for two days each in the trenches, two on duty at the guns, two for visiting the wagon-line, and for resting or as odd-jobs officer, a number varying according to the number of subalterns available. This number varied from one (myself) at the beginning of January to five at the end of February, when we had Withers, Denvir, Murray Lyon, Campbell, and me. Campbell, however was with us only a few weeks, and was then posted to 'D' battery.

But the normal number was three, as there were generally one or two of us on courses or on leave, and so our 'week' was a six-day one – two days in the trenches, two at the guns, and two at the wagon-line.

My week began on the morning when, after an early breakfast, I went down to the trenches to relieve the previous FOO. A number of different hours were tried, but 9 a.m. was eventually fixed on as the most suitable time for these reliefs.

Before he left, my predecessor would tell me all about anything new or interesting during his term of duty. Then I would go and make my bow to the company commander in his ramshackle mess or still more ramshackle sleeping-place in Trench 70, and, if the weather was very thick so that observation was impossible, spend most of the morning with him.

In fine, clear weather I would spend my time in one of the bays of the trench, searching through a periscope or, on occasion, with my eyes over the top of the parapet, for any movement behind the enemy's lines. A telephone wire connected my bay with the battery, and I always had a telephone and telephonist with me, so that, if I saw anything worth firing at, I could get the guns on it without delay. If the enemy shelled our trenches at all, I would get the guns firing on his front line in retaliation, and by this means, as we always fired four times as many shells as he had done, we soon taught him to leave us alone. While it had sometimes happened that as many as a hundred shells fell in Trench 72 in one morning during the autumn, when we covered it, it was seldom that he fired more than two or three rounds in a day into our present zone, so much had we increased his respect for us.

I used to have meals with the company officers in Trench 70, and in the evening we would sit in the mess – a draughty sandbag affair, with two of its corners blown out – or in the company commander's dug-out. The latter had a beautiful brick fire-place, and commanded a fine view of the lake – a wide stretch of thick green water. But the side opposite the fireplace had been blown in by one of the enemy's trench-mortar bombs, crushing the iron bedstead, and the water of the lake used to flow in at the door, and cover the floor to a depth of half a foot.

Owing to the new policy of 'defence in depth' – i.e. placing your troops in a series of defensive lines instead of all in the front line, where they would probably all be destroyed in the enemy's first rush – and to the flooded state of the country, which made an enemy offensive almost impossible, the authorities had now (end of February) adopted a different principle of holding the line. The front line was not nearly so thickly held as of old – one could walk for hundreds of yards without meeting a sentry – and the infantry got more rest. Every company in the division, I think, did a two-day tour in Trenches 70 and 71, which were much the worst in the sector. One platoon held the Mushroom and the crater saps, two held Trench 70, and one Trench 71. As they were in that part of the line for so short a time, the infantry naturally, did little work on the parapets and earthworks which soon began falling to pieces as the sandbags rotted and collapsed.

The state of the trenches, then, grew worse and worse. Here and there the duck-boards lost themselves in big ponds, like the green lake already mentioned and the larger sheet of water between Trench 70 and Trench 71 supports. The sentry post at the extreme northern end of the Mushroom was cut off from the rest of the trench and from the communication trench leading to Trench 70 by a broad expanse of water known as the 'Blue Lagoon'. The 'lagoon' was mostly about knee-deep – waist-deep in places – and consisted of thick, greenish water, quite opaque. In the slimy mud at the bottom lay the bodies of innumerable rats and of an unknown number of men, who had been wounded during the December fighting about the craters and, sticking fast in the mud, had been drowned.

There was no dry ground. The sandbags with which the breastworks were occasionally repaired were filled with the filthy ooze dug out of the 'lagoons', and contained much decaying matter – bodies of men and vermin, spoilt and abandoned tins of bully beef and biscuits, rotting sandbags used in previous constructions, broken and decayed fragments of equipment and clothing, and the contents of the 'middens' of the battered farms and all but vanished cottages which lay around. An odour of putrefaction enveloped the whole place.

Worst, perhaps, of all was the FOO's dug-out. In the dry weather of the early autumn it had been a pleasant little place, with brick steps leading down from the duck-boards of the trench. Now it was very different. The brick steps had slipped down into the dug-out, leaving a slope of slimy mud, down which water ran in from the flooded trench. There were 6 inches of water on the floor – so many inches of solid ice during the cold weather of February and March. There was a stove which would not burn, a broken table, and a rickety wire-netting bed, on which the seeker after sleep was perilously poised above the thick black water. The bed was only about 4 feet long, but a hole in the wall enabled one to stretch out one's legs until one's feet, well outside the dug-out, came in contact with the duck-boards of the trench. So placed, they were liable to be trampled on by all passers-by – who, even while doing their best to keep clear, would slither off the wet, tilted gangway on to them – and were exposed to the inclemency of the weather. I used to sleep with my feet in sandbags, often with four of them on each foot – an illegal proceeding, in view of the shortage of sandbags – and more than once I have woken up in the cold grey of a winter's dawn to find 6 inches of wet snow on my feet. Under these conditions we spent two nights in four, six, eight or ten, as the case might be. I generally managed to get a certain amount of sleep – I am not sure that the others did. Unpleasant as they were, I suppose that it was these nights, and the experience which I gained under these conditions, which taught me to make the best of everything, and to endure cold, fatigue and discomfort with such equanimity as I did later on.

After two days and nights passed in these circumstances I would be relieved. It is worth noting, in passing, that the period of my tour and the conditions under which I lived in the trenches were identical with those of the infantry. I had to be on duty for forty-eight hours at a stretch, and on the go continuously from the dawn 'stand to' to the end of the evening one. I was liable to be called out at night on every occasion on which they were called out – any alarm, for example – and on many occasions on which they were not called out – whenever our guns were doing any close-shooting, or to 'spot' the flashes of any enemy guns or the positions of any searchlights, lamp signal-stations, etc., which might be in action during the night. In one other respect, indeed, I was worse off than the infantry: I received no rum issue to warm me and no whale oil to keep my feet free from frostbite. Nor, of course, had I one of the steel helmets which were now being issued to infantry snipers, but which were not yet known to us. In view of all this, and of the fact that these trenches, in whose discomforts we shared, were the worst which the infantry of the division was ever called upon to hold – except, perhaps at Flers in October 1916 and Ypres in October 1917, when the lot of the infantry was admittedly better than that of the artillery – I do not think that anyone can accuse us of sitting at ease in the background while the infantry suffered and fought for us in the front line trenches. It must be admitted that our job, though, perhaps, usually safer than theirs, was certainly not more pleasant – and on some fronts, as I have already pointed out, it was more dangerous and more unpleasant.

The infantry certainly appreciated our presence in the trenches. Owing to another change of system, the 8th Lincolns had a long spell in Trenches 70–71, and we soon learned to get on with them as well as we had done with the other battalions of the 63rd Brigade. With one battery covering each company, we got to know one another very well – an excellent thing for, as all the text-books assure us, the success of any operation involving co-operation between two arms is made much more certain if the officers concerned are personally acquainted.

If there were only three officers available for trench duty, the day on which one was relieved in the trenches was usually one of those on which one visited the wagon-line, the idea being that the relieved officer – who had not washed or shaved for two days – could go down and have a good clean-up at the Pont de Nieppe baths. If there were more than three, it was set apart for 'rest'.

As a matter of fact, I seldom went down to Pont de Nieppe, as I preferred a bath in front of my own fire. There was plenty of coal in the abandoned houses, and I had a roaring fire whenever I wanted it, and bathed in front of it in a large wooden tub. When I had had a bath, shaved, and changed my clothes, I would have lunch, and then ride down to the wagon-line, returning usually for a late tea, which was followed after an interval by supper, perusal of intelligence summaries, orders, etc., to the accompaniment of a gramophone, and an early retirement to a bed where I slept between sheets on a soft mattress.

We used to get in a good deal of sleep in those days. The officer on duty at the guns had to be on parade at 9 a.m., when all the men paraded and were inspected before starting work. But the remaining officers seldom came in to breakfast before ten o'clock – a good twelve hours after they had retired the night before.

A day on duty at the guns was not a very strenuous affair. At 9 a.m. the officer on duty inspected the men at the gun-line, to see that they were shaved and that their buttons and boots were polished up, etc. Then he used to walk round the position and see that the guns were clean, and everything was tidy, etc. If the FOO in the trenches wished to use the guns, the officer on duty at the battery had to be present when they were fired, and the same applied when any 'programme shoot' had to be carried out, whether by day or night. He was also supposed to supervise gun-drill for the men, all of whom were, of course, only semi-trained, but this was usually allowed to lapse.

Most of the firing was done about 3 p.m., as the light was usually at its best for us during the afternoon, and we always tried to do our shooting at a time convenient to the infantry. They usually liked us to get it over by tea-time, and we chose the hour of three o'clock as being one when we did not interrupt either their meals or our own. Of course, if targets appeared in the morning, or if we had any 'programme shoot' – bombardment or barrage preparatory to or covering a raid – we had to depart from our usual timetable.

Each officer spent two of the six days of his 'week' at the wagon-line. One of these days – usually the one on which he came out of the trenches – he treated as a rest day. He would ride down in the afternoon, bathe (if he had not already had a bath at his house), do any necessary shopping for himself or for the mess, and go to Lucienne's or the 'Au Boeuf' for tea.

The other day he took more seriously. He would arrive at the wagon-line for stables at 11 a.m., stay there until the end of stable-hour, see that the men got dinner, etc., and go on to lunch with the 'column' at Nieppe. The column used to give us excellent stew and, as all their officers had been in 'C' battery at different times, we were always welcome.

He would return to the wagon-line after lunch, and spend the afternoon there. There was always a certain amount of work to be done. At one time most of his time was spent making peace between the QMS and the Farrier QMS, a specially enlisted Army Veterinary Corps man attached to the battery, who, though incompetent to perform his own job, thought it his business to run the wagon-line. In the end he was had up for 'when on active service, drunk' and striking his superior officer – the QMS – and was court-martialled. Most of the light punishment he received was remitted by the convening officer, but, anyway, we were rid of him.

Having stayed at the wagon-line until the end of evening stables, the officer would ride home for tea, or sometimes feast in the town and get home for supper. Then next morning his week would begin again, and he would go off to the trenches.

And that, with only slight variation, was our routine week after week. We were at the height of trench warfare in its most concentrated form. It was a kind of fighting unknown in previous wars, a kind which induced habits of sluggishness and loss of initiative which it took the British army many months to shake off. For us, however, it came as a welcome period of careful nursing after our collapse at Loos.

4
THE SOMME, 1916

Preparation

The battery detrained at Longueau, east of Amiens, in the afternoon on 1 April, and marched to Bussy-lès-Daours. It was a long march, and we watered at the river en route. We got into camp after dark. The lines were in a wood of eight-year-old poplars – they afterwards claimed 45 francs for damage done to these – and the officers and men had billets in the village. Two officers – Withers and I – slept in the attics of the château with some of the HQ officers, but we all messed together.

We had a very good time at Bussy. The weather was fine, and the horses grew fat. Amiens was close, and many went there, but I was not one of them.

The first wet day was the 11th, when the left section, preceded by me and accompanied by Murray Lyon, marched to Dernancourt, on the Ancre, and established its wagon-line in a grassy bog known as 'Stephenson's Field'. After dark we relieved a section of the 12th Battery Royal Fleet Auxiliary (7th Division) in an old French position above Becordel. I do not know whether it is the usual procedure with regular batteries – the 12th Battery pulled out before we arrived, and left no one to hand over.

It rained continuously. At the gun position we were not too badly off, for we all had dug-outs. And all except the mess, where Murray Lyon slept, were waterproof. But at the wagon-line things were very miserable. The horses occupied a little island in the Ancre marshes, and were never above their hocks in mud, but the men, accustomed to luxurious billets at Pont de Nieppe, had only a very wet bank in which to dig, and little material of which to make bivouacs. I got them a certain amount of corrugated iron etc., but by the time it was forthcoming in any considerable quantity we wanted all we could get for other purposes.

On the 15th Dalton came up from Bussy, and we held a council of war, at which we learned definitely for the first time – it had long been rumoured – that the 21st Division had been picked out, with some others, to deliver the first blow of a great offensive which was imminent. We were to build a strong position forthwith beside the bridge by which the Albert–Péronne road crossed that from Becordel to Becourt, and from this position we were to do our share in the preliminary bombardment. All was to be ready by the 27th.

That afternoon we made all speed to get the position marked out. Eleven more gunners arrived from Bussy in the evening, and that night we started work. We had one gunner wounded by machine gun fire, and after that we worked by day.

We did not get on very fast. We kept on 'indenting' for material, but the Royal Engineers failed to supply it. To obtain props for the gun-pits we had to cut down all the telegraph poles from Bellevue farm to the crest above Fricourt. We also had recourse to less honest means. While Sgt Porter removed occasional bits of timber from a Royal Engineers dump just opposite, Sgt Jones, under cover of darkness, carried away wagon-loads of 9-inch by 3-inch timber from the Corps dump behind Meaulte.

One day Sgt Porter was caught. The Chief Royal Engineer (CRE) came along to me in a passion and, with a sapper armed with a tape measure, proceeded to measure all the timber in the place. He even broke into a hermetically sealed ammunition pit which we had built – we had put on the roof before we cut an entrance. As a result of his labours, he found that only about 5 per cent of the timber in our possession had been legally come by, and he went away muttering curses and swearing that we should soon hear all about the other 95 per cent.

A day or two later General Jacob, the GOC Division, came round, and, on hearing my name, expressed intense displeasure. Next day Dalton came up from Bussy with whole sheaves of papers, including a report from the CRE and a request by Division for my 'reasons in writing'. To this, at Dalton's suggestion, I made a spirited reply, pointing out that the CRE's own report – in which he described his dumps as being subjected to 'petty pilfering' – proved the utter incapacity of the divisional sappers, and Dalton backed me up. The end of it was that I was told not to do it again, and a divisional routine order threatened future pilferers with severe disciplinary action. But I think the CRE was 'told off' as well, for from that day forth he was very polite, and returned my salutes with pleasant smiles.

Just about time, Dalton having gone on leave, Denvir brought the right section into action at Bellevue Farm, where it was attached to A/94. I came into contact with Weil, who was acting OC while his major was on leave, and he reported me to his colonel for being rude to his signallers. However, as both Denvir and the signallers took my side, his report was discredited and the victory lay with me.

My section was tactically under the OC 94th Brigade Royal Field Artillery, Col F. M. Bannister. It was a 'close defence' section, i.e. we were to keep quiet until the enemy attacked, and then continue firing at him till captured. On one occasion we were told that a big attack was imminent, and had to register various points on his front line. There was a great 'strafe' that night and, thinking that the moment had come, I dashed off in pyjamas and gum-boots to my OP, only to find that nothing was happening.

A day or two later, while I was away at Bussy, the enemy loosed a gas-cloud. As always when emergency demanded their presence at the telephone, the whole of the 94th Brigade HQ stood gaping in the High Street at Meaulte, and let the instrument buzz in an empty house. When at last he got through, Murray Lyon obtained the adjutant's permission to fire nineteen rounds on his SOS lines – which he did, only to be severely strafed by the Hun in reply the next morning.

We got on badly with the 94th Brigade, and not much better with the 95th (Lt-Col M. E. Fitzgerald) which relieved them later on. Coates had left us at Bussy, and Major J. L. Courtney was now in command of the 96th Brigade, all of which, except 'C' battery, was still at Bussy. Each battery had a party building its 'strafe' position, and these parties were all attached to us for rations etc.

We were sorry to lose Coates, little though we had liked him while he was with us. We played a football match in the château grounds to celebrate his going – he played goal for one side and Courtney for the other. It was reported that B/96 offered their green Flemish farm cart, drawn by two long-maned mules, to convey him to the station.

While not so actively unpleasant as Coates, Courtney was the type of interfering incompetent whom we particularly disliked. Further, he feasted at A/96 all day and was in the habit of reeling homewards across our position about six o'clock every evening.

In the middle of May the authorities did away with the brigade ammunition columns. This reorganisation was the prelude to another one – one which concerned us more intimately. At noon on 20 May A/95, B/94 and C/96 became known respectively as A/97, B/97 and C/97, and formed a 97th Brigade of three 18-

pounder batteries under Lt-Col E. C. Pottinger and the old 97th (Howitzer) Brigade HQ staff. The result of all this was to give the division three artillery brigades corresponding to its three infantry brigades, each comprising a headquarters, three four-gun 18-pounder batteries, and one four-gun howitzer battery.

The change made little difference to us. Our wagon-line moved from the southern to the northern side of the wood in the valley east of Dernancourt. The guns remained in action in the same positions, and we went on working on our 'strafe' position at Becordel.

I went on leave on 27 May, and, by the time I got back, the position was almost finished, and the right section had been brought down from Bellevue Farm and installed in its new pits. The position comprised four gun-pits with concreted roofs about 4 feet thick, joined to one another and to a series of ammunition pits by a slit-trench, the whole lying on the north side of the embankment of the Albert–Péronne road. On the south side of the road a second trench connected up the officers' and men's quarters with the cook-house etc., bathroom, and a further series of ammunition pits. The two trenches were connected by a tunnel some 60 feet long under the road, with three mined dug-outs opening off it.

We had a series of wet nights in the middle of June, and this was the time chosen to fill up with ammunition. Lorries from the direction of Bray brought it up, and were liable to arrive at any hour of the night. I think it took four nights to get in our establishment of 3,000 rounds.

All this time the left section was in the position taken over on 11 April. It did little firing. The infantry carried out a few raids but with no great success. The enemy had one big success against a battalion of the 34th Division on our left, but the situation was saved by the 1st East Yorkshire (21st Division). On two parts of our front – the 'Tambour' and the 'Purfleet' – the enemy made great use of the heaviest '*minen-werfer*', causing many casualties among our trench garrison. An ambulance stood always by our position ready to receive the wounded.

For the most part the weather was fine, and, under these conditions, the country towards Albert, Meaulte and Ville-sous-Corbie was very pleasant. In case of an enemy offensive breakthrough before our offensive began, it was intended to hold the line of the Ancre, and reserve positions were reconnoitred about Buire.

All through June orders were pouring in. The change to Summer Time caused many of them to be amended. The preliminary bombardment, which was to prepare the way for our attack, was to begin on 24 June and last five days. Early on 29 June the attack was to be delivered. Advancing in company with the divisions on their right and left, the 7th and 21st Divisions were to attack the south and west faces of the enemy's Fricourt salient. The village itself was not to be attacked: the two divisions were to join hands beyond it, at Bottom Wood, and cut it off. Fricourt having fallen, the advance was to be continued in a north-easterly direction.

On 20 June we moved the left section into the new position; on 22 June we fired a few rounds registration, and then we were ready for the bombardment.

The Bombardment

The bombardment started as soon as the light permitted – about 5 a.m. – on 24 June, the first round in our area being fired by C/96 and the second by C/97. The day was given over entirely to wire-cutting – that is to say, to destroying the enemy's barbed wire entanglements with shrapnel etc., in order that they might present no obstacle to our attacking troops. So thick and so numerous were the entanglements that to destroy them alone, several days' continuous bombardment was necessary. The night and, after 25 June, the greater part of the day was spent in bombarding the enemy's lines, communication trenches, strong points, tracks, roads, light railways, dumps, head-quarters and gun positions.

The 21st Divisional front extended from Fricourt to South Sausage Redoubt. The enemy's country was divided into four strips running at right angles to the front, and each of the four artillery brigades was responsible for the destruction of the wire and trenches and the bombardment of all important points in one of these strips. As far as I remember, the order of brigades from right to left was: 94th, 96th, 97th, 95th. A howitzer battery of the 17th Division was attached of the 17th Division was attached to the 97th Brigade RFA.

The concentration of artillery, heavy as well as field, was many times greater than any concentration ever seen or thought of before, and the expenditure of ammunition, not only during the bombardment but also during the two preceding days, which were employed by all batteries in registration, far exceeded anything previously imagined. After the first few hours the hostile batteries, overwhelmed by the weight of the bombardment, became completely silent.

During this period the artillery was the most important of all arms. The infantry, also, were doing their share. The divisional front was held by the 62nd Infantry Brigade, and, besides discharging clouds of gas and smoke, when opportunity offered, they carried out several raids, and patrols were constantly out by night, reconnoitring and reporting on the state to which we had reduced the enemy's trenches and wire.

While we were thus exerting ourselves on the ground, the Royal Flying Corps had obtained complete command of the air. With the exception of a certain amount of night flying in May, the enemy's planes accomplished nothing. From the middle of April to the middle of July our aeroplanes were up always, in all weathers, and scarcely a single German appeared above our lines.

C/97 fired about 1,000 rounds a day, and my job of supervising the ammunition supply kept me busy. Not only was I responsible that there was always sufficient ammunition on the position, but also it fell to me to see that each gun was kept supplied with the same type of ammunition as its neighbour for each bombardment, that enough ammunition was always available close to the guns, that the ammunition was always kept separated according to its nature, and that, if any one nature of ammunition ran out and another had to be used, suitable corrections were put on the guns.

Having all this to do, I only got up to the OP once during the preliminary bombardment. On this occasion I went up to Work 18, south of Becordel, and from there cut the wire in front of Crucifix Trench, using two guns firing section fire, thirty seconds. The CRA congratulated me on cutting this wire effectively.

We were equally successful with the wire along Gin Alley, but the thick, heavy masses before South Sausage Redoubt proved very difficult. Here there was a dense accumulation of rusty wire on long stakes and 'high rests' many yards thick, and, to add to our difficulties, we could shoot at it only in enfilade. On the last night of the bombardment the authorities, thinking that we had failed to cut a lane, sent a party of sappers with a Bangalore torpedo to blow one. Fortunately for our reputation, on arrival before the enemy's front line, they found that, not only had we successfully cut a lane, but we had so effectively destroyed the entanglement that there was no wire left for them to blow up.

All this time we kept up our bombardment upon the enemy's communications, whereby we prevented his trench garrisons from receiving rations and ammunition. At the same time our heavies knocked out his guns – our counter-battery work on the Somme was better than it ever has been before or since. Nothing but the enemy's numerous deep dug-outs saved his harassed troops from complete annihilation.

The attack was fixed originally for 29 June, and the attacking brigades – the 63rd and 64th – were moved up to the trenches the preceding evening. At the last moment, however, the final attack was postponed for two days, and the two brigades were brought back to their rest billets. This would appear to have been done solely for the purpose of discouraging our men and of giving the enemy more time to bring up his reserves. I have never heard any reason for this postponement.

At last the evening of 30 June arrived, and the attacking brigades were again moved up. At a council of war in the mess Dalton allocated the duties for the morrow. He and Darling – a new subaltern who had joined us at Bussy – would be at the OP and Denvir at the guns. Murray Lyon was to cross No Man's Land in rear of the attacking infantry and get a line through to a forward OP somewhere near the Dingle. As second in command of the battery, I was to go down to the wagon-line to bring up the teams when required.

As it happened these plans were very nearly brought to nothing at the very moment when they were announced. We were all in the mess, sitting and standing around, and talking to Dalton, when the Bosch fired one of his short bursts on to the road across our position. One of his shells struck a tree which grew up through the mess, breaking it off a foot or so above our roof. The shock was tremendous, our two candles went out, and we all instinctively dived under the table. After a few moments, as no more shells came, we crawled out, re-lit our candles, and resumed our plan-making.

Fricourt and Mametz Wood

I rose early on the first of July, and, after an excellent breakfast of fried eggs and bacon – Darling was mess secretary – I rode off towards the wagon-line. At 7.30 a.m. the attack was delivered, and stray machine gun bullets hummed around me as I rode. I found Meaulte full of soldiers lying all over the footpaths – men of the 62nd Brigade and the 17th Division, waiting to go up. All the villagers were standing at their doors gazing into the east, where a dense and acrid smoke, mingling with the morning mist, lay stretched along the skyline marking the field of battle.

At the wagon-line everything was packed up, the teams were hooked in, and we were prepared to move at any moment. We knew little of what was going on. Late in the morning an Indian trooper arrived, escorted by a runner belonging to the Somersets, desiring Sgt Ince to dress a wound on his horse. The runner told me that the Somersets had had very heavy casualties, and he thought the Middlesex had too. Every now and then I sent an orderly up to the guns to get news, but we gathered little except that we had certainly advanced. There seemed little prospect of the guns going forward that evening.

Having taken up ammunition in the evening, I remained at the guns for the night, and there learned more or less what had happened. The attack had been delivered at 7.30 a.m. On the divisional front it had been made by two brigades, the 63rd on the right and the 64th on the left, each with two battalions in the front wave and two in the second. Simultaneously with our attack a small force – I suppose a battalion – of the 17th was to make a demonstration before Fricourt, in order to keep the Germans occupied until the 63rd Brigade got safely over No Man's Land. Unfortunately this force started half an hour too soon, entered its own artillery barrage, and was destroyed.

The result was that, when the 21st Division attacked, the garrison of Fricourt was able to concentrate its attention and its machine guns on the 63rd Brigade From their position they were able to enfilade it as it advanced, causing it very heavy losses. By the time the Somersets – who were on the right – reached the enemy's front line, the battalion had practically ceased to exist, and the Middlesex on their left were in little better case.

Our troops had apparently advanced a long way in some places, but had come back to a more definite line, as on the right the enemy still held Fricourt and the communication trench leading up to it from the neighbourhood of Bottom Wood, and on the left, also, the situation was obscure.

The next day, also, I spent at the wagon-line, expecting to be called upon at any moment. Fricourt was to be attacked at 11 a.m., and it was expected that, once the village was taken, progress would be rapid. Nobody at the wagon-lines had any information about anything, neither Reid of 'B' battery nor the Regimental Sergeant Major. I don't think A/97 had an officer down there. We all expected to go up with the teams very soon.

There was much traffic on the road between Meaulte and Ville-sous-Corbie, troops and ammunition going up, ambulances and prisoners going down. The balloon which usually floated over the wagon-line had moved up as far as the Royal Engineers dump at Meaulte. A 12-inch gun on railway mounting at Dernancourt fired regularly, and nearly blew the horses off their feet at each round, but otherwise little of the battle was to be heard.

We received no order to advance. On returning to the guns at nightfall, I was told that the garrison of Fricourt had come out and surrendered an hour before the attack was to start. Nevertheless the rest of our line had not advanced appreciably. On the left the enemy still held the Boisselle: two battalions of the 34th Division had got into Contalmaison and had there been surrounded and destroyed by the enemy. The rest of the division had made little progress, and the divisions to the north of it had made none. On two thirds of the front attacked on 1 July we had been severely repulsed: only the 21st Division and those on the right had made progress. On the other hand, the French on our right had made a striking advance, but it must not be forgotten

71

that the positions which they attacked were not nearly so strong as those which lay before us.

I spent two more days at the wagon-line, and at the end of that time, deciding that no sudden move was likely, we no longer stood-to by day. A/94 had advanced from their position at Bellevue Farm on the 1st, but were still at Becordel on the 3rd. Eventually they came into action near Lonely Copse, beyond the enemy's front line north of Fricourt.

On the 5th, I went with Denvir in the evening to look at Fricourt. An occasional gas shell burst over the road, but otherwise all was very quiet. The mutilated trees raised broken limbs above a scene of utter desolation. Hardly a wall stood. Bricks, timber and household furniture blocked the road. The debris of war – abandoned rifles, bayonets, haversacks, water bottles, coats, boots, gas-helmets, bombs and many 'dud' shells and broken shrapnel bodies – covered the ground. Deep shell-holes lay on every side. Here and there a deep, dark hole marked the broken cellar of what had been a house.

We walked through the village, where the passage of British troops had worn a pathway through the ruins, and came back by the old German front line. Here the destruction was even more complete. Whole acres of ground had been so ploughed and ploughed again by our shells that not a blade of grass remained, nor was there any sign of the trenches which had been there. I went into one, which was nicely panelled in white wood – it had been an officers' dug-out – with neat sliding doors concealing shelves for cups. The place had already been rifled, and I found only a small book, which I took but afterwards lost.

No one who had not seen it could have imagined that the power of artillery was so great. A week's bombardment had reduced many acres of pleasant country to a howling desert – the most desolate evil-smelling desert it is possible to conceive.

I went away convinced that the artillery was the arm that would win the war, and that nothing could stand against us.

Next morning I was called at two, much to the indignation of Muskett, who was a lazy fellow, and went up to observe. I took Bombardier Stephenson with me and, finding the farrier sergeant wandering about searching for a forge-cart in Fricourt with Pegasus, commandeered that unlucky mascot to carry wire as far as the Dingle.

I went up to Black Tree Wood, where we found many bodies, including those of Headlam's brigade major and others who had fallen when the general led his celebrated attack on the wood. In Shelter Trench were a few German bodies. I sent Stephenson back to guide the wire up, and went forward into a shell-hole overlooking Contalmaison.

No sooner had I arrived than the enemy put eighteen 4.2s over my hole, so I went back to Birch Tree Trench, and selected a position about 18 inches deep, from which I obtained a wide view comprising Contalmaison village, the villa, Pearl Wood etc., High Wood and Mametz Wood.

We did not get the wire through till 4 p.m. After carrying out some registration, I was called in, just as the rain started, and went home along the road built across the old trench systems by the divisional engineers. On this occasion Stephenson, so far forward for the first time, fully justified my recommendation of him for appointment to Bombardier in June. We got in at dark, and I settled down to a most acceptable supper of scrambled eggs on toast.

For the next three days it rained almost continuously. Not only was infantry action suspended, but the position became full of water. The communication trenches, which were poorly revetted and had suffered from the rain on the 4th, began to fall in and, as no one had time to look after them, got full of water and became impassable. Even the tunnel was wet underfoot, but, though unrevetted, the walls showed no sign of collapsing. The officers' mess, badly sited under a roadside ditch, was perhaps the wettest of all.

I was in the OP again for the next big show – at Bois Francais this time, in an old German trench. At dawn on the 10th the 38th (Welsh) Division attacked the southern and eastern sides of the wood, advancing in many cases, each comprising a line of, I suppose, platoons in artillery formation, untroubled by the Hun. Our troops lined the edges of the wood, where a number were hit by shells, and pressed on inwards. Inside, I believe, the fighting was very bitter. Reinforcements continued to enter the wood well on into the afternoon. About lunchtime a British aeroplane crashed in the eastern arm of the wood – the first I had seen brought down.

At 5.30 p.m. a heavy concentration of artillery opened on Contalmaison, whose houses, though damaged, still stood. The village, taken and lost by the 34th Division on 1 July, had changed hands twice since then, and was now in those of the enemy. In an hour we had reduced it to a few little heaps of bricks and some mutilated trees which raised appealing arms around the shattered remains of the château. Then the infantry attacked the village from the west and south. We could see the bursts of their bombs moving steadily eastwards through the village. Finally, just at dusk, they emerged at the eastern end, and pressed out as far as the Cutting. For the third time Contalmaison had been taken, and this time it was held.

I retired to bed in a little dug-out behind the OP, but about 10 p.m. I was recalled to the gun-position as the battery was moving. Reeling in the wire as I came, I arrived hot and flurried, only to be told that the move had been postponed.

By this time, of course, a certain amount of progress had been made on the left. La Boiselle and, I think, Ovillers, which had proved insuperable barriers to the 34th and 8th Divisions, had been taken, but further north no more attacks had been attempted. On the right little progress had been made: they were waiting for us. By capturing the Quadrangle System, Mametz Wood – which was finally cleared of the enemy by the 21st Division, now back in line, on 11 July – and Contalmaison, we had won ourselves a strong position immediately in front of the enemy's second main defensive system – that which covered Longueval and the Bazentins – and had made it possible to bring up the guns for the bombardment of this line.

Bazentin and High Wood

I have always held that the policy of attacking which we pursued on the Somme, that of going for limited objectives with comparatively small numbers of men, and then consolidating them, is not only the most costly which could have been invented, but is such as to render victory impossible. The efficacy of our artillery preparation and the heroism of our infantry were thrown away under a wooden system of attack which throttled all initiative. Terrified of again losing all as by the first wild forward rush at Loos – a rush which, though it did, in fact, cause disaster came very near being a complete breakthrough and giving us an overwhelming victory – the authorities decided to take little at a time and to make sure of it, and so confined our infantry to miserable 500-yard advances, which cost them very heavily and achieved nothing. It is my opinion that, by so doing, our own staff definitely thwarted our New Armies of victory on the Somme.

I did not realise this at the time, but we all had glimmerings along these lines that something was wrong. The easy breakthrough and rapid pursuit that we had foreseen had not taken place. The advance, which we at the wagon-line had expected at any moment on the first day, did not take place until the 11th.

On 11 July, in the evening, we came into action before Railway Copse. Shelter Wood was on our left front, Bottom Wood on our right. 'A' and 'B' Batteries were on our right – their approach had been spotted by a kite balloon and the enemy had put a 5.9 barrage across the mouth of the valley, destroying one of A/97's teams. Sgt Porter, also, narrowly escaped destruction.

Dalton and Darling repaired early to the OP at Pommies Redoubt, whence they directed our fire – we were taking part in the bombardment of the enemy's second system. This system, to which Quadrangle formed a bastion, consisted of a double-line of deep trenches, furnished with dug-outs and machine gun emplacements, both steel and concrete, and running in front of the fortified villages of Longueval, Bazentin-le-Grand and Bazentin-le-Petit, to Pozieres. In front of each of the three villages lay a wood which was full of trenches and entanglements, and very thick. Taken as a whole, the system – trenches, woods and villages – was of very remarkable strength, especially as observation on it was difficult.

I ran things at the battery end. On the 12th I sent Denvir forward to find out where our line was etc., and he seems to have spent his time walking up and down the road in front of the enemy's position, counting the broken limbers which strewed it. Next day they called for a list of men recommended for awards. Several names were sent in, including Murray Lyon's, but none received anything.

The rest of the wire was cut comfortably on the 13th, and at dawn on the 14th the attack was launched. I was at the guns for the bombardment, Denvir being at the OP. In a few hours the whole show was over. Our infantry, forming up in the semi-darkness in front of Mametz Wood, had carried the enemy's position and the wood and village of Bazentin-le-Petit almost at a single rush. Though the enemy evicted them at least once from the village, they quickly recaptured it, and that night advanced their line to a road beyond it.

After the bombardment I went to bed – we all had beds in an old German dug-out of great size and depth. For about an hour the enemy kept me from sleep by putting gas shells at the dug-out entrance – the first I had seen – and so it was late when I awoke to find everybody in great excitement. The cavalry was astir. Denvir had spotted large numbers of them moving on High Wood.

It seemed at last as though the great moment – the great opportunity – had come. And so it had, but, apparently owing to the lack of initiative, or the inability, owing to their orders, to use it, of the local authorities, it was missed. The cavalry went up to High Wood, but what they did there no one knows. Anyway, they very soon came out again with a few prisoners, and bore them off miles behind the lines.

To our great disappointment, it soon became clear that the cavalry had achieved nothing. We had infantry there, it was true, but as we had failed to take Longueval or to make any progress on the left of the 21st Division towards Pozieres, their position was precarious. In fact on the night of the 15th/16th they were withdrawn to positions covering the Bazentins.

On the 15th I went out to look around. After getting lost in a thick mist, I found friends at 110th Infantry Brigade HQ in Mametz Wood. Poor General Hessey was in a state of great excitement. An ill-expressed order from Division had caused him to retire his brigade from Bazentin-le-Petit wood, leaving it almost empty. Apparently only the mist concealed this from the Bosch, who failed to step into the gap, and, by good fortune, it was closed up again and nothing was lost.

This 110th Infantry Brigade had joined us from the 37th Division to replace what remained of the ill-fated 63rd Brigade, and became from this time onward an integral and a distinguished part of our division. But in the opinion of the old friends of the 63rd, it was but a poor substitute for General Hill's gallant brigade.

It was to visit the Leicesters, troops of the 110th Brigade, that Farrell of A/97, Stitt of B/97 and I set out from Mametz Wood. We had an interesting but hardly an exciting tour. The most interesting feature of all was lunch, of which we partook at 7th and 9th Leicester battalion HQ – just the corner of a trench where the two colonels squatted with their two adjutants. Their rations had miscarried, and they were overjoyed at the sight of a camp pie which I produced and a bottle of wine brought out by Farrell. When we went away, we left several tins of bully which we had been carrying, and set out with lightened pockets, and minds lightened, too, by the knowledge of well-doing, towards Bazentin-le-Petit village.

I got home very tired, only to be once again prevented from going to sleep by gas. This time the shells were not near me, but the gas, of a type new to me, was very strong. The sergeant major was bathing in a shell-hole, and narrowly escaped gassing. We had no casualties. 'A' battery, I believe, had one, but their gas discipline had always been bad.

Before I leave it, I cannot resist again drawing attention to the fact that the capture of the Bazentins by the 7th and 21st Divisions, after only a short bombardment, and in the face of an enemy who had had time to bring up troops and guns, was a very notable achievement.

But now an entirely new problem confronted us. Despite the ubiquity of our aeroplanes, they had only just perceived – or the information had only just percolated through to us – that the enemy had constructed a new trench – the celebrated Switch Trench. This trench ran from a point south of Martinpuinte, along the north side of the crest, through the north-west corner of High Wood, and crossed the Longueval Road at a point south of Flers, where it connected up with the enemy's old third system. Throughout its length this trench ran along the northern side of the crest, and no part of the trench itself and only a very small length of its wire was visible to ground observers on our side.

Obsessed by the idea that a prolonged artillery preparation was necessary, and cramped, I suppose, by the failure of the attack of the 14th on the right and left, our staff hesitated and was lost. Instead of throwing large forces against the unfinished entanglements and half dug bays of Switch Trench, they contented with a few very small attacks on the south side of the crest, and directed us to prevent work on the Switch Trench system by keeping it under fire. Unfortunately, owing to lack of observation, to the inability of the Royal Flying Corps to register our guns, and to the continual small movements of our infantry, which inclined us to shoot long for safety, our fire on the trench was not well enough directed to stop further work on it, and the enemy soon had a powerful fortified line drawn across our front.

On the 18th/19th I was acting as liaison officer with the 98th Infantry Brigade (33rd Division), which was then in our sector of the line. During the night men of the Middlesex regiment captured a German artillery officer in Bazentin-le-Petit wood. Ever since the 14th, he had remained there, well behind our lines, directing by means of a telephone and buried cable the fire of his batteries on such targets as he could see. His position commanded the long valley on the eastern side of Mametz Wood, where infantry brigade HQ was, and here he had caught the 96th Brigade RFA advancing into action, and had inflicted heavy casualties on several batteries. He was wounded when taken, and had with him telephones and maps. What happened to him eventually I do not know.

The 97th was to advance to positions in front of Mametz Wood, chosen by Pottinger from a distant position of security above Sabot Copse. I went there on the 19th, and found that they were under observation from several square miles of Bosch country on our right, where he still held ground well in advance of Switch Trench. As a result of a report to the same effect by Major Nanson of B/97, the idea of moving to these positions was abandoned. We therefore remained in the Railway Copse valley, where we at least had made ourselves very comfortable in our underground palace – where every man had a bed and several units besides ourselves found lodgings – firing at extreme range at Switch Trench – a process which our buffers would not stand for long. Broken springs were frequent: I think I am right in saying that, at no time after moving to Railway Copse, did we have more than three guns in action. Even so, we did better than other batteries, who carried on for days at a time with two, or even one in action.

By this time the enemy must have had all his reserves up. The prospects of a breakthrough seemed remote. His guns were heavies and much more numerous than on, say, 6 July. His aeroplanes were now cruising in fleets of a dozen or so, and, though cautious, enjoyed great liberty of action, being apparently too numerous for our airmen to tackle. The result was that the enemy's shelling, besides increasing in volume, improved in direction and became really unpleasant.

At dawn on 23 July, after an all-night bombardment, we launched our first serious attack on the growing fortifications of Switch Trench. On the right, or east, of High Wood troops of the 5th Division entered the enemy's positions, but were ejected. On the left the attack was made by the 51st Division, which attempted to advance in no great strength over a very wide and open No Man's Land, and was mown down in the process. Here, as on several occasions in the Arras fighting in 1917, we carried to absurdity our usual fault of attacking with too small forces. It has always seemed to me that, while it may save losses at the time, this process inevitably prolongs the fighting and causes us more casualties in the long run, besides, in combination with the 'limited objectives' folly, definitely rendering decisive victory impossible.

I spent the morning of the 23rd in an OP above Bazentin-le-Grand and, having made a tour of the front line in the afternoon, returned to the battery at dusk, only to find that we were to be relieved next day. That day the enemy placed at least one very heavy concentration, chiefly of small shells, on the Bottom Wood area, causing casualties in the wagon-lines immediately to the right of our guns.

At 4 p.m. on the 24th, having handed over our ammunition to the 256th Brigade (51st Division), which, however, did not occupy our positions, we pulled out. On this occasion I moved the whole gun-line, with all the officers' mess and telephone stores, on four gun-limbers. We went out through Fricourt, paused for tea at the wagon-line, which was still near Becordel, and went on that night to Bonnay. We arrived long after dark, to find all arrangements made for our comfort by Major Nanson, who had got in by daylight – consideration for which we were very grateful to him.

So ended, for the present, our share in the disappointing but glorious Battle of the Somme – the first great fight of the New Army.

Flers and Geudecourt

It was a long time since any action had been made on the most important section of the Somme front, and our line still ran almost as it had on 24 July, on the southern face of the High Wood ridge. The enemy still held Switch Trench, now a formidable system, almost on the crest, and visible from no point in our front except, possibly, from Ginchy, recently captured. Advances had been made on the right, but all our efforts against Switch Trench had resulted in fruitless sacrifice of men.

Just as we arrived on the scene again, however, a new spirit began to appear – the old spirit of 1 July, the old confidence in immediate and decisive victory. The cause of this rise in 'moral' was the appearance of that new and powerful weapon, the tank. Early in May, while on leave, Dalton had met an officer of the Motor Machine Gun Corps, who had told him of some new and invincible armoured cars, for whose arrival the offensive was being delayed. But, beyond that, we had heard nothing of any new weapon, and we had long forgotten Dalton's story. So it came as a great surprise to us to find all the troops in Albert agog with excitement about the tanks. These monsters, which had only just arrived upon the scene and had been seen by few, were described as of fabulous size and of two kinds, 'female', armed with machine-guns, and 'male', armed with 6-pounder – or, as some said, 6-inch – guns.

The first tanks I saw were close to the ruins of Mametz when taking up ammunition on the afternoon of the 14th. They were standing above the road, covered with camouflage sheets, and the soft mud of the bank was churned with their tracks. It was very late when I came back, and I met them coming up the wet road towards Bazentin – unwieldy monsters, clanking slowly forward, much to the inconvenience of other traffic, as they took up nearly the whole road, and the horses, meeting them in the dark, shied all over the place. Three tanks there were – going to take up their positions for the great breakthrough attack on the morrow, when, in the forefront of our assault, they were to storm Switch Trench.

I did not get to bed that night. It was dawn when I got back to the new wagon-line at Mametz, and an all-pervading thunder, accompanied by the smell of burnt cordite and thousands of primrose flashes in the misty valleys, announced the beginning of our attack. There we stood on the crest, gazing into the north, smelling the battle, and waiting for orders and the first sign of victory.

White was there. He was the senior officer in the wagon-lines, and took charge when we moved up to the eastern side of Mametz Wood to be at hand when the batteries should have to advance. When the teams were called for, it took us a long time to get up to the guns, though so near, owing to the great crowd of forward-moving traffic on the roads and the shell-ploughed state of the ground, which precluded all movement across country.

When I arrived at the position, Wood went on ahead to find the next one, and, having limbered up, I led the battery along the road towards Delville Wood. The leading battery – the whole brigade was advancing in column of route – found itself unable to cross the wet, shell-ploughed country between the Longueval road and the High Wood crest, and we had to wait on the road until a track could be made. This took some time, and I was in constant fear that the enemy would turn his guns on the road, in which case the blocked traffic would fall an easy prey. Several shells fell quite close, but none on the road, and after a while we were able to move forward. A guide took us along a track across a valley to the left of the road, and the guns went up into action by sections, followed after an interval by the wagons, which dumped their ammunition, some on the position, some short of it.

I stayed in the valley and collected the teams under cover. Shells fell here and there, but none on us. Three tanks, their work finished, came lumbering over the hill, causing consternation among the horses. Eventually, having collected all the teams and the empty limbers and wagons, I led them, as fast as decency and the traffic would permit, towards Mametz. Part of the road, by the way, past Bazentin-le-Grand wood, was paved entirely with British 8-inch 'duds', which were very numerous.

I had some difficulty in finding the wagon-line, which was neither at Mametz Wood, where we had been in the morning, nor at Mametz, where I had left the front-line wagons at dawn.

In the end I found it about half a mile from the latter place, on the Montaubon road, where it had gone by order of Brigade HQ.

I arrived very late and went to sleep under the GS wagon, promising myself a late breakfast, as I had not been to bed at all the night before. Quite early, however, an orderly woke me: he had a note from Hawes, informing me that Wood had been wounded, and requesting me to come up and take charge.

This I did, arriving at the gun position just as a barrage was being fired. I sent Hawes down to the wagon-line, and ran the show until tea-time, when my old friend Captain Johnstone, now second-in-command of C/96, arrived to take command.

That evening he and I walked up to our OP above Flers – a somewhat shell-swept spot – and next day to see if we could find another in Delville Wood. The same day Major McGowan was wounded, and Johnstone left us to take over C/96, which contained a section of his old battery, A/96. C/95 liked Johnstone as much as could be expected, seeing how little they had seen of him, but thought that he walked too far for them, and too fast.

Dalton relieved Johnstone in command of C/95. He attempted to rule the men as he had ruled C/96, but, accustomed to the iron hand of Wood, they proceeded to take advantage of what they imagined to be his weakness, and his rule was not a success. At a later date I tried the same experiment, and the result was the same. He got on very well with the officers, and Eaton even built a mess with his own hands – a thing, he said, which he would never have done for Wood.

I stayed at the guns, Hawes at the wagon-line. Up till the 16th it had been fine, but after Dalton took charge we had several days continuous rain. We had little material to make ourselves shelters, the mess was thoroughly bad, we fired almost continuously, and the rain washed out many limbs and bodies which had been buried in the all-pervading sticky yellow mud. Altogether these days were some of the most dismal I have ever spent. There was not a leaf or a blade of grass near the position: the ground was an uninterrupted sea of mud, ploughed up over and over again by heavy shells, and full of deep water-filled craters. It soon became quite impassable for wagons, and the ammunition came up on dripping pack-horses, which slithered into shell-holes and dug-outs and could only be got out after an hour's work. Rations were bad, casualties frequent, and the men's work was enormously increased by the necessity of carrying up to the position the ammunition dumped by Wood on the 15th some hundreds of yards in rear. And all the time we kept on firing on to the mist-shrouded country in front, 'harassing' the enemy.

By the 23rd, however, it had cleared up to a certain extent, and an attack was planned on Gueudecourt and the strong trenches in front of it, known as Gird Trench and Gird Support. We fixed a barrage but, owing to all the runners being either bogged or killed, the attack failed to materialise. Some days before I had been down to Flers to select a position for a forward gun, but had been unable to find a good one, and the idea of pushing a gun forward was abandoned. On this occasion I had seen and admired the New Zealanders, who then held the western part of Flers and the front to the left of it. Various divisions, whose numbers I forget, were afterwards put in in that sector.

At this time we covered the 55th Division, which held the front to the right of Flers. Between them and Lesboeufs was the infantry of the 21st Division, supported by the artillery of, I think, the 5th Division. Next to them were the Guards and, on their right, the French, who had extended northward. At this time, of course, the idea of an 'allied generalissimo' and of 'inter-penetration' of armies were non-existent, and French and British each had their own definite area.

One day while Dalton was in command Arthur Blackden came to supper on Crowse's invitation. A few days later he was killed in front of Flers. He was with a battery of the 41st

Division, under whose CRA, Brigadier General Lushington, we were serving.

On the 27th, the 21st and 55th Divisions again attacked Gueudecourt. Creagh of C/96 and I were to follow up the attack and fix up telephonic communication between the new battalion HQ and our own HQ (C/95 was attached to the 95th Brigade).

The attack was delivered in the afternoon. Setting out from C/96's OP in Fish Alley about 2 p.m., we proceeded through Flers, where we narrowly escaped destruction by an 8-inch shell, Creagh being wounded on the finger. After much wandering about and dispatching of orderlies, we got a line laid about nightfall, but failed to get through on it. On this trip we discovered a woman's clothing in a German dug-out at Flers, but failed to find a much more important thing, viz. a gun-position in the vicinity. Long after dark I went up with Bombardier Wickham to Infantry Brigade HQ, which was established in a derelict tank near the Flers road, and from there cut homewards across country. Guiding myself by a star, I described a complete circle, after which I deemed it prudent to follow the road, and got home very late.

The same day, just before I left the battery, we had been surprised by the sudden arrival of Wood's valise, and, shortly afterwards, of Wood himself. Wounded less seriously than at first supposed, he had got as far as Étaples but, afraid to go to England as it would involve loss of acting rank, he insisted on returning to the battery. His return was not altogether welcome. Dalton stayed on for a day as second-in-command of the battery, and then went off to C/94, which was very short of officers. It was about this time, also, that Telfer was posted to that battery.

Just about this time some spare batteries of the 94th and 96th Brigades were pushed forward to Flers, where they occupied very exposed positions and suffered heavy casualties. C/94 had to leave their guns for some days, and lost many men, including

Cpl Scott killed and Sgt Mackrill wounded. C/96, with other batteries, was in action to the west of Flers, on the High Wood side.

On 1 October the New Zealanders attacked Eaucourt l'Abbaye. Wood and I got a good view of the battle from Switch Trench. On the right they appeared to encounter little opposition, and passed over the ridge towards Ligny-Thilloy throwing smoke bombs in front of them. On the left, however, they appeared to be held up by machine-gun fire, and two tanks were sent up to help them. As frequently occurred at this time, the attack was delivered in the afternoon, and dusk prevented our seeing what happened when the tanks arrived on the scene of action.

On 2 October Captain Johnstone was killed. He had gone out without his body-shield, contrary to custom, and, while he was in one of the pits, a shell had burst, wounding him in the stomach. A stretcher was found, and he was carried towards the next dressing station, but he died in Switch Trench before he arrived. His last efforts, I believe, were instructions to Primrose as to the battery. And thus, doing his duty to the end, passed away one of the bravest, kindest, most chivalrous and at the same time most unfortunate men that I have known.

Next day Crowse and I were reconnoitring for possible positions to the west of Flers, and visited Timson and Primrose at C/96, and found them much grieved, as well they might be. Dalton arrived that evening to take command of the battery.

We did not move down to Flers after all, but remained in our shell-torn wilderness in front of Delville Wood. The guns had been well dug-in and we were less conspicuous to the enemy's balloons, of which as many as fourteen were visible on most days from the pits. Our aeroplanes used to go over sometimes and drop incendiary bombs on them, causing great white masses, like inverted shaving brushes, to hang in the sky. Speaking generally, however, our command in the air was not nearly so secure as formerly, Bosch aeroplanes crossing our line in great numbers on fine days.

Every day or two we delivered fresh attacks. Not very far from our front line lay the red roofs and green trees of Ligny-Thilloy and the hamlets beside it, and on the crest behind arose the towers of Bapaume – a picture of peace contrasting oddly with the mined villages and leafless trunks arising out of the brown shell-tossed earth on our side of the line. But we never reached these tempting goals. Deep in the mire, our infantry struggled on by successive stages as far as the so-called 'Brown Line', a sort of indefinite trench line on which the enemy finally held up our attackers. By the middle of October the Battle of the Somme was over: we had achieved much, but we had definitely failed to break through.

On the 13th three guns of a battery of the 29th Division – possibly the 92nd or 97th Battery RFA, but I am not certain – arrived to relieve us. We had no use for them. The officers boasted continuously of their achievements at Gallipoli and of being regulars. As a matter of fact, we had more regular officers in C/95 than they had, and their battery was the most 'ragtime' show I have met. The right-half battery came out of action with Crowse and myself.

After a night's rest at the wagon-line, we marched to La Neuville, a suburb of Corbie. I do not remember much about it, except that I saw Shrine – formerly of the 8th Somersets and now of the Trench Mortars – in Corbie, and we had a most excellent dinner at, I think, the Hotel de la Poste. Next day the rest of the battery joined us at La Neuville.

We were not very sorry to see the last of the Somme. The division had won much honour, and had been warmly congratulated both in July and in October by the GOC-in-Chief Fourth Army and the GOC XV Corps. But we had paid for it. The 94th Brigade had had many casualties and, in the attack on Gueudecourt, our infantry, especially the 64th Brigade, had lost heavily owing to the wire not being cut. At that time, I think, the 5th Division Artillery was covering our infantry. We were supporting the 55th Division, who thanked us warmly for our help. We had a very high opinion of them: for one battalion, particularly, with which I was doing 'liaison' on a night when a powerful counter-attack was expected and all the SOS rockets were found to be wet, I have the greatest respect. Later, unfortunately, our zone was shifted further to the left, and we found ourselves 'liaising' with (among others) the headquarters of the 165th Infantry Brigade, and I desire to place on record the cavalier fashion in which they and the other Brigade HQ staffs treated artillery liaison officers.

The battle was over. Desultory fighting went on and, in November, blazed up again for a few days in the Battle of the Ancre, but by the middle of October serious fighting was ended. We had failed to break through, but we had accomplished a number of smaller things, which Sir Douglas Haig enumerated in his dispatches. But our losses had been beyond computation. This was the last great effort of the British voluntary army, and it had left it so weak that conscription had become a necessity. Restored to its former strength, and increased by the addition of conscripts, the army was never again what it had been on 1 July. Every man of that great host had come forth voluntarily to serve his country in her need, and I feel sure that no army which Britain has ever placed or will ever place in the field could be more formidable. Whatever causes may have brought about our failure, no one can hold our soldiers and regimental officers in any way responsible for it. To their invincible spirit was entirely due such measure of success – not altogether negligible, either – as we did achieve.

5
STALEMATE, 1917

It was some time since we had first heard of the enemy's retreat from his positions south of Arras and from the line on which he had finally held up our offensive of 1916. If only our troops of the Third, Fifth and Fourth Armies could press on fast enough to prevent him organising a resistance on the 'Hindenburg Line' – a prepared system of enormous strength which was believed to exist some miles behind the positions which he had abandoned – and to 'keep him on the run', we might yet drive him back across the Rhine. It seemed likely that at last the unfulfilled dreams of Loos and the Somme were about to materialise, and that the end of the war was in sight.

The road from St Pol to St Michel was crowded with lorries and buses – a continuous stream of laden vehicles hurrying troops eastward to the scene of our advance. Far into the night the lorries rattled down the cobbled road with their human freight. The main road through St Michel was lined with heavy guns of all calibres with their tractors, most of which before morning had gone off after the lorries.

We arrived in St Michel shortly before dusk and sat down on a log in the snow while Melle sought out the Town Major. It was quite dark and snowing hard before he got back and showed us where to put our men and horses for the night. Bain – a most inveterate seeker after the whiskey bottle – and the other members of the party went off to St Pol, while Melle, Crowse and I climbed a steep hill during a blizzard and found a lodging in a cottage at the top. After shaving ourselves in the kitchen, and consuming between us an omelette of thirty-two eggs prepared by our hospitable hostess, we turned in and slept.

At 9 a.m. we met the Town Major and the rest of our party – some of whom, finding no accommodation in St Pol, had spent a frigid night on the balcony of an iron foundry – and did our billeting, led by the Trench Mortars at a gallop along roads many inches deep in sticky mud.

The brigade pulled in after lunch, and we spent the next night in the village – quite uneventful except that Crowse went to sleep over a rubber of bridge, and was severely strafed by the major. An officer of the divisional train, whose name I forget, messed with us.

Early next morning the billeting party pressed on to Lucheux, followed more leisurely by the brigade. Here we found that we were expected to make ourselves comfortable in some bleak and by no means snow-proof huts set down on a bare slope of mud.

The day of our arrival was fine, but next day it snowed hard. A large amount of very war-worn artillery guns drawn chiefly by teams of about four mules and hardly one officer per battery – passed our camp in a northerly direction. They were army brigades which had wintered in the knee-deep mud of the Somme and had been present at the taking of Irles and the entry into Bapaume in the first stages of the advance. Their numbers I forget; one brigade bore a fox on its wagons.

On the 26th we received orders to march on the following day. I rode into Doullens to purchase a few oddments – underclothes, boots, etc. – and to have a bath. Before leaving Lucheux we had to reduce our kits to 35 pounds per officer in anticipation of rapid movement, our surplus being dumped at Moudicourt.

The Battle of Arras

We fired almost continuously every day of the bombardment. Our ammunition allotment was not great – nothing to what it had been on the Somme – but there we had been in the middle of the battlefront and here we were on its southernmost fringe. Day and night the guns roared to the north, and the ground shook to the reverberations of a bombardment to which that which paved the way for the Somme offensive had been child's play.

All the while the weather grew worse. The rain which had fallen for several days changed to snow, which fell more or less continuously. The blast-marks and the quivering nets above the guns stood out black on a snowy hillside, intersected only by tracks made by infantry wagons, lost in the murk.

Every evening the teams came up with ammunition, the emaciated horses panting and toiling through the snow. The strain was too great, and many of them dropped in their traces from sheer exhaustion. The whitened landscape was littered with the bodies of these our faithful servants, who had fallen, toiling till they dropped. Alone of the batteries of the division, C/95 lost no horses. One battery is said to have lost as many as 120 out of an establishment of 173.

The wagon-lines at Ayette must have presented a terrible spectacle. Every morning at least a dozen dead horses were found in the lines of most of the batteries. How any survived on their meagre ration I do not know.

If the horses' rations were meagre, those of the men fell even further below the usual standard. For several days there was hardly anything to eat at all, and for several days after that we lived each on two-thirds of an iron ration. The officers, unable to buy their accustomed luxuries, felt the shortage even more than the men. We complained bitterly, forgetting that for several miles in rear of us every railway had been demolished and every road rendered impassable by the enemy, and that it was, in fact, evidence of the great efficiency of the Army Service Corps that we got anything to eat at all.

The country surrounding our position was in fact a desert. Boyelles lay to our left, Hamelincourt in rear, and St Leger to our right front: in these three villages hardly one brick stood upon another. Ruined houses and their contents lay strewn across the roads. In front of us stood the embankment of the Boyelles–St Leger railway, but the rails had been uprooted and carried away, and not even a sleeper remained on the track. On our right a huge mine crater blocked the junction of the road from Hamelincourt with that from Boyelles and St Leger. Beyond it rose the stark ruins of Judas Farm. Across the Hamelincourt road lay rows of trees – once it had been an avenue – felled across it by the enemy to hinder our advance.

In view of the complete destruction of all communications, the rapidity of our advance reflects great credit on the staffs concerned, and on the engineer units which opened up communications with so little delay, and the administrative services which kept us supplied with necessities under the greatest difficulties. The greatest praise is due to the artillery and, even more, to the infantry for the speed with which they followed up the enemy and the dash which they displayed in the fighting in front of the Hindenburg Line in the worst possible conditions of weather and lack of shelter. The hardships suffered by the infantry during these days defy description.

Easter Sunday, 8 April, was a fine day. The sun shone out of a blue sky on a country clad in dazzling white. The great attack on the Hindenburg Line had been fixed for this day, but had been postponed until the afternoon of Monday. General Wellesley came round the batteries on that day to wish us success.

By this time 'A' battery had moved forward to the Henin–St Leger road, and C/94 had moved into their vacated position on our left. B/95 also went forward in the evening to a position near the Henin–Croisilles road. Our position had become more or less habitable. The mess consisted of a hole in the bank covered with a waterproof sheet. It was furnished with a table – on which the major slept – and a plush-covered seat – found among the ruins of Boyelles. Crowse and I slept in an adjoining hole, roofed like the mess. Hawes slept there too intermittently, but most of his time was spent at the wagon-line, as he suffered from boils.

We woke early on the 9th to find snow falling out of a leaden sky. To the north the guns were thundering their support to the Canadians attacking at Vimy. The snow fell continuously. Gradually division after division took up the battle, and the thunder of the guns came ever louder and nearer, until at 4 p.m. it came to our turn.

The 21st Division, at this time the right division of the Third Army, was to form the southern flank of the attack. The 64th Brigade, attacking in support of the division on our left, was to occupy part of the Hindenburg Line south of the Cojeul and the high ground towards Wancourt Tower, while the 110th Brigade was to extend its front in order that, while its right flank remained stationary at Croisilles, its left flank might be advanced in conformity with the forward movement of the 64th Brigade.

The barrage was put down shortly before 4 p.m. and ceased at 4.45 p.m. Preceded and screened by it, the 64th Brigade was to breach the enemy's line. The heavies had been responsible for cutting the wire, especially the 6-inch howitzers with their new 106 fuze, but only one gap had been made, and that not by the heavies at all, but by A/95. The infantry, advancing with great dash, swept through this gap, overran a portion of the enemy's front and support lines, and established themselves therein, but failed to advance further.

At 8 p.m. or thereabouts the enemy counter-attacked, coming forward during a blizzard which drove the snow into the faces of our troops. The SOS barrage was promptly opened, and was maintained for about half an hour, at the end of which time we were ordered to stop firing. The enemy's attack had been partially successful, and he had succeeded in ousting our troops from some of the trenches which they had taken in the afternoon.

Confused fighting followed for some days. The 56th Division worked their way along that portion of the Hindenburg Line lying between the Cojeul and the point where we had breached it on the 9th. Troops of the 21st Division and, subsequently, of the 33rd Division, which relieved them about the 12th, extended our original gains bit by bit southwards along the Hindenburg front and support lines, descending towards the Sensee valley, but little or no attempt was made to advance northwards or eastwards.

For the first time in my experience, we had had our own wireless mast, and responded to aeroplane calls on our own responsibility. As, however, we were now a long way from the front line and could cover only a small area behind the enemy's positions, our usefulness as a 'counter-battery' was not very great. Several hostile batteries were, however, engaged by us on receipt of aeroplane calls on the 9th and 10th.

Early on the 11th we received orders to advance. Wood was away at the time, but on his return set out again at once through the snow to reconnoitre a new position. We pulled out at nightfall, by which time it was snowing heavily, and moved up across the railway and along the valley across the Henin–St Leger road to a position beside 'A' battery. It was snowing hard the whole time and Eaton had much trouble in getting the limbers and emptied wagons back to Ayette. Many horses fell down on the way and died from exhaustion. Others reached the lines, but were dead by the morning. Counting eight which were sent to 'mobile' on the following morning, we lost thirty-seven horses that night – our first loss, and probably the heaviest sustained by any battery in a single night.

During the night we dug the guns in and erected camouflage over them. I laid out the line during the most violent part of the storm by 'individual angles', holding a torch on the director and one on the sight. The officers' servants had made some tea, with which we washed down a frugal meal of bread and sardines, standing wrapped in our greatcoats in the falling snow and using the water cart as a table.

The servants were then set on digging a dug-out in the bank of the road, while we went over to see to the digging-in of the guns. Returning – frozen through – at 1 a.m., we found that the major had taken possession of the dug-out as a bedroom for himself. Further, he charged us in no measured terms to return to the position and work on until the dawn. About 4 a.m., all work being now finished, we routed out our servants, and made them spread our beds in an open trench, the snow having ceased to fall.

We slept for half an hour. Then Wood roused us and sent Crowse off to look for an OP. For breakfast, sardines and tea. Our table was an ammunition box set in the middle of the road, and we stood round it. The snow lay smooth on the ground, and a pale sun shone feebly from a yellowish sky. Only one black figure moved to and fro over the whitened waste – Bombardier Kettle, laying a wire to the OP. A painfully slow process it would have been too, had not the major roared at him at intervals and galvanised him into spasmodic action.

A colonel of the Leicesters had lent the major a German periscope-director, found in a captured OP above Croisilles, and so pleased was he with this toy that his temper improved considerably, and at lunchtime Watson and I plucked up our courage sufficiently to venture into his dug-out, only to be

Above: 1. Artillery on the Lens Road.
Right: 2. Commanding Officer Meeres, Royal Field Artillery.

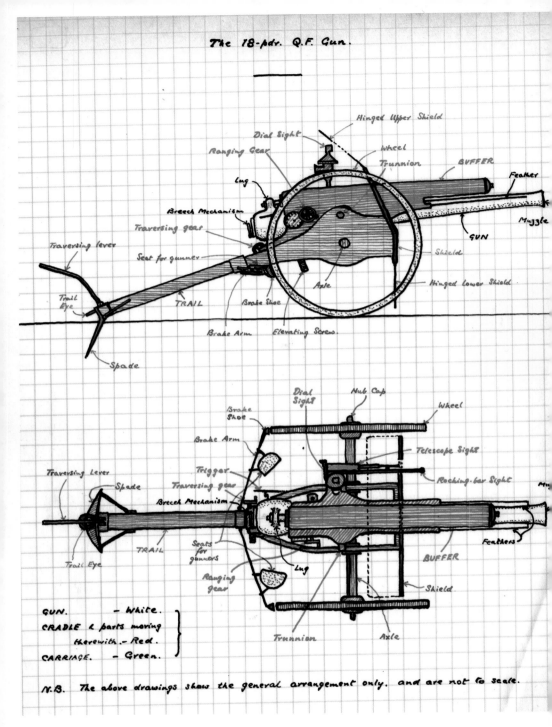

3. The eighteen-pounder gun.

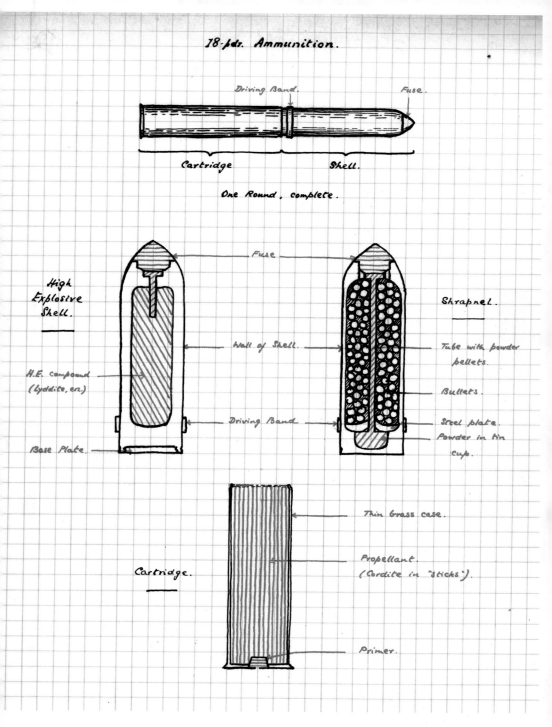

4. The ammunition.

5. Night on the Western Front.

6. Guns at night.

7. A communication trench.

Above: 8. Meeres in France, 1918.
Right: 9. At the trenches, 1916.

Above: 10. Annequin Fosse.
Left: 11. Place Notre Dame,
Armentières.

Above: 12. Guns going into action.
Right: 13. Albert.

Opposite top: 14. On the Somme.
Opposite bottom: 15. Dawn in the trenches.
Above: 16. The Somme, September 1916.
Below: 17. April snow in Flanders.

18. The Battle of the Somme.

Left: 19. Arras.
Above: 20. Forward Observation
Officer in action.
Below: 21. Péronne.
Opposite top: 22. Searchlights.
Opposite bottom: 23. Croisilles.

Opposite top: 24. Lieramont.
Opposite bottom: 25. The advance on the Ancre, August 1918.
Top: 26. Night at the guns.

27. Château du Bois le Duc.

Above: 28. Meeres and friend, 1916 or 1917.
Right: 29. Precautions against gas, 1916.
Below: 30. On horseback, Berkhamsted, 1915.

31. 'Stripes', H. J. Parsons riding, 1915.

informed in tones of icy politeness that 'this was not a mess'. Greatly incensed, we began forthwith to construct an abode for ourselves, and by evening it was roofed with a waterproof sheet and ready for occupation. This dug-out was used as mess and sleeping-place by Crowse, Watson, myself and, on his return from the wagon-line, Hawes. The major slept and fed in solitary state next door.

The feud lasted for several days. On the 23rd of the month troops of the 33rd Division delivered their long-talked-of attack on that part of the Hindenburg Line which remained in the hands of the enemy, but made little progress. I believe that a slight advance was made eastwards on the high ground towards Chevisy. This village, by the way, was never captured by us, and remains to this day in the hands of the enemy, though claimed, I believe, in one of our official communiqués.

During the day a 5.9-inch howitzer shelled D/95, which was in action on the road close to our dug-outs. Only one of their men was killed, the remainder being withdrawn owing to the large number of gas-shells on the position and the danger of their being exploded. Major Daynes came over to our position, slightly cut about the face.

The shelling continued all day, the 5.9s all passing over our heads and falling in 'D' battery's position and among the heavies nearby. During the afternoon a number of 4.2s fell in and about our position, but did no damage, and we continued firing. One 5.9, however, fell on the Major's dug-out and demolished it, burying his kit.

After this the major tired of living alone, and a new mess was built in a bank above the battery. This mess commanded a fine view of the valley, which was full of batteries of all calibres. Behind us was a battery of 8-inch howitzers, and behind D/95 a couple of 6-inch hows. A little further along the road, behind A/95, were four 9.2-inch hows, and beyond them another 4.5-inch battery and some 60-pounders, while on the St Leger side was a 13-pounder battery. With the 8-inch firing battery fire every 10 seconds and the 9.2s firing salvoes, and all the smaller fry going as hard as they could, no inconsiderable clamour rose from our valley. On a German counter-battery map dated 22/4/17 which I saw later, all these positions were shown as active.

One day Wood and I went to the OP – a trench beside a sunken road north of Croisilles – and fired many rounds at the enemy's trenches astride the Croisilles–Fontaine road. From here we commanded the Sensee valley and Fontaine-lès-Croisilles. The Hindenburg Line – this portion of which was still in the hands of the enemy – ran just in front of the village and continued up towards Buttlecourt. The portion already captured by us lay to the north of Fontaine, the village and wood remaining in possession of the Germans.

On another occasion, when the major was at the OP alone, a shell landed on the parapet of the trench and blew him out of it, knocking his glasses out of his hand and burying them. Search parties went up from the battery daily after the event for several days, and demolished the OP in looking for the glasses, but never succeeded in finding them.

Our troubles were over now. The weather was still cold and often wet, but there was no more snow, and towards the end of the month summer broke in upon us. The wagon-lines had moved from their swamp at Ayette and were now installed at Hamelincourt, the remaining wagon-lines of the brigade being in the valley immediately below Moyenneville.

Since the attack of the 23rd, the 21st Division had again come into the line. For the moment comparative peace reigned, but we continued to shell the Hindenburg Line – two broad white bands stretching up across the green from the Sensee towards Bullecourt. It was understood that another attack, bigger than any that had gone before, would be delivered on a very wide front in a few days, and the cavalry which – disappointed of their expected breakthrough on 9 April – had retired behind the scenes, was once again in evidence. A few tanks were also concealed in posts of vantage behind our lines – a sure sign in those days of something about to happen.

Summer at Croisilles

On the 26th, three days after the attack by the 33rd Division, Crowse's section moved into an open position between the Sensee and the railway, immediately south of Croisilles. The two guns were installed by night and camouflaged, and soon after dawn on the 27th commenced cutting the wire before the Hindenburg Line over open sights. Only one point in the parapet of Bing Trench – the front line of the Hindenburg system south of the Sensee – was actually visible from the guns, but the enemy's wire entanglements stretched right across the crest about 1,500 yards in front of the position, so situated that it could be cut effectively with percussion shrapnel observed, if desired, from the guns.

Our zone had gradually slipped further to the right, and now lay to the south of the Croisilles–Fontaine road. Hitherto only that part of the Hindenburg Line which lay to the north of the river had been attacked, but the great blow of 3 May was to be delivered on the whole front of the 5th and 3rd Armies and on part of the First Army front. The 21st was the right division of the Third Army, and stood astride the dry ditch known as the Sensee River. On our right was the Fifth Army and next to us, immediately north of Bullecourt, the 7th and 62nd Divisions.

On the 27th the remainder of the battery moved up, arriving at Croisilles shortly after dusk and digging in before dawn. The position being visible from the enemy's wire, only the guns and signal-pit – the latter an old drain under the railway embankment – were on the actual position, the officers and men being in sunken roads some hundreds of yards to the rear and across the railway. Two men slept in each pit to fire the gun in case of any emergency.

The cold weather had gone for good by this time, and it was fine and gloriously warm. The change was very welcome, and we basked in the sun with infinite enjoyment. Hawes had been on the wagon-line, but on 1 May he came up, and I went down there for ten days' rest. I found Eaton living in an old French summer-house on the east edge of Hamelincourt, and the horse-lines and gun-park all laid out in a smooth green field close to divisional headquarters. A pleasanter spot for a wagon-line could hardly have been chosen.

On 3 May the great attack was duly delivered, and resulted in a deplorable fiasco. On 23 April Wood had seen the infantry of the 33rd Division giving themselves up, scores at a time – going over to the enemy with their hands up. On this occasion things were little better. The 110th Brigade (21st Division) penetrated as far as Fontaine Wood, but was hurled back by the enemy. In the resulting confusion our men lost their heads: many surrendered or fled, losing all that they had gained.

Nor was this all. A crowd of men wearing bandages on their heads and arms ran back through our gun-position until stopped by the major at the point of the revolver. He made them take off their bandages and ascertained that none of them had in fact been wounded. He therefore drove them back towards the front line, covering them with his revolver until they were out of sight lest they should again attempt to retire. To what regiment these men belonged I do not know.

But the 21st was not the only division which failed on that day. By nightfall, despite the enormous expenditure of ammunition and the heavy casualties sustained, no unit of the three armies which had attacked stood in advance of the position which it had occupied before the battle took place.

Ypres

[Meeres was in hospital in England for much of 1917, suffering from trench fever. He thus missed the Third Battle of Ypres, but heard about it from his colleagues.]

The brigade had been two months at Ypres, engaged in that struggle for the ridges known as the Third Battle of Ypres. I had missed it, but from the descriptions of survivors and from my experiences of the infinitely more pleasant and infinitely less terrible Battle of the Somme in the autumn of 1916, I could picture it.

Never before had artillery been massed as at Ypres: never has it been since, nor ever, I imagine, will it be again. One of our barrages, for instance, covered with bursting shells the whole of the enemy's position to a depth of 1,500 yards right round the salient. That while it was stationary. When it began to creep its depth increased to 2,500 yards – a contrast indeed to those frail curtains of fire, only 200 yards deep, behind which our infantry had gone out to their death on the Somme.

But, despite the power of our artillery, our casualties were infinitely greater at Ypres than at the Somme. Hampered by the mud, going forward at less than 25 yards a minute because of the heaviness of their equipment and of the ground, our men fell easy victims to the expert marksmen who garrisoned with machine-guns their shell-proof 'pill-boxes' – little concrete forts, hard to hit because so small, hard to break open when hit because so strong. Can one wonder that British infantry – not, as far as I can hear, of the 21st Division – their nerves already shattered during their passage through the terrible back areas of the salient, refused to advance against the enemy?

I have referred to the terrible back areas. Even in the autumn of 1916 the infantry admitted that they would as soon be where they were as in the gunners: at Ypres they thanked heaven that they were infantry. The front line was a haven of refuge compared to the shell-torn mud flats where the guns were. Our batteries were so thick on the ground that, fire where he would, the enemy could not fail to hit one. Never before has such an enormous quantity of artillery been massed in a small space as it was both sides at Ypres.

On the Somme there had been roads – some of them, as at Bazentin, had been paved with shells, others, like the Flers road, with the bodies of men and horses half-buried in the mud, still they were roads. At Ypres there were no roads. The wide swamps of desolate mud could be crossed only by 'corduroy' tracks – built-up roadways of wood, which the enemy gunners knew to a nicety. Hundreds of lives must have been lost in maintaining these tracks, which were shelled and destroyed as soon as made. Wounded animals, staggering over the side of the roadway, were engulfed in the surrounding mud and perished by starvation or suffocation. Doubtless men moving alone on the less frequented tracks met with the same fate: it was a common thing for men to go out and never return or be heard of again.

It was in the midst of this that the batteries had to live. They fired day and night. While at Ypres A/95 lost over twenty guns by direct hits and some twenty men and many horses. The wagon-lines were bombed every night. How anyone ever came out of Ypres I cannot understand.

6

THE GERMAN ADVANCE, SPRING 1918

Preparations for Defence

Ever since Cambrai rumours of a great German offensive between Cambrai and St Quentin had been current. It was expected in March. While out of action we had reconnoitred a series of positions as far back as Aizecourt-le-Haut to be occupied in case of a retreat. Our own troops and Italian labour companies were busy building lines of defence and putting up wire entanglements.

From Gauche Wood to the eastern end of Epehy the front was held by the 21st Division. On our right was the 16th Division, on our left the 9th Division. These three divisions, English, Irish and Scottish, and the best representatives of each, formed a very stout corps. We were all in the VII Corps, commanded by Lt-Gen. W. Congreve VC, who had taken over the corps when General Snow went back to England, and had his headquarters at Templeux-la-Forse – a most unhealthy spot constantly bombarded by enemy aeroplanes. The VII Corps formed the extreme left of the Fifth Army (General Gough), which held the whole front from Gouzeaucourt to La Fère and had its headquarters at Nesle. Immediately on the left of the 9th Division lay General Byng's Third Army.

We covered various zones. At first we had fired towards the Beet Factory and Villers Guislain, and used a very shaky barn in Peiziere as an OP. Later our zone lay more over to the right, and we used to observe from a concrete tower among the ruined buildings of Epehy. Near this OP we had a gun which was supposed to deal with any hostile troops which might appear when the offensive was launched.

I was back at Longavesnes for three weeks or so. The weather was improving. There had been much snow in December and January – on Christmas day we had seen the green grass for the first and last time for some weeks, during which it was covered with a mantle of ice and snow. February was wet but, as a whole, the winter neither so wet as our first nor so cold as our second. And it seemed curiously short. By the middle of March the fine, warm weather had come, and it stayed with us for quite a long time. Though we had more snow well on into April, the winter was really over by the time I went on leave.

Snow or sunshine, rain or gale, the long, low, lonely hills stretched out on all sides the same as ever, broken only by scattered leafless woods, by lone trees, spared by the retreating Hun, which raised their lonely heads into the stormy sky and tossed their arms as though calling for their comrades ruthlessly destroyed, and by the ugly outlines of British camps and Nissen huts and the wet mud sites of empty horse-lines. It was a desolate country indeed, this waste of silent down-land, rolling away, ridge after ridge, to the flat horizon. Somewhere to the west the green hills of this empty land melted into the crimson, shell-torn crests of the Somme battlefield, where the scarred yellow earth was now clothed with a red weed. The weed grew high round the lonely crosses in those silent valleys, it enveloped the broken walls of ruined villages, and it wrapped in a mantle of old those sad hill-sides which had been watered for five long months with the best blood of the three greatest peoples in the world. The great battlefield slept, untouched by man, alone with its sorrows and its glory.

But the downs of Longavesnes were changing. Night after night the aeroplanes came over dropping bombs in all the ruined villages. Day after day men, British and Italian, toiled in the making of lines of defence. The green hillsides were scarred with the light-brown lines of new trenches. Entanglements sprang up in a night, so that it was dangerous to ride after dark lest you should become involved in one. Heaps of white grass on green chalk marked the presence of mined dug-outs. Day and night the once silent country was full of the sound of marching troops, horsed and motor transport on the roads, trains passing on the railways, aeroplanes droning overhead, and tanks passing to and fro to their stations under cover of darkness.

Then we began to hear rumours. A German aeroplane had been brought down, and on the pilot's body were found orders for an attack on 3 March. All that night troops passed eastwards through Longavesnes. At length came the grey dawn. We strained our ears to catch the first sound of battle. Our 'heavies' were going but that was all. There was no attack that day.

My leave was due on 16 March. I hardly knew what I wanted to happen. I did not want to miss the battle, but nor did I want my leave delayed. Then, one day I went to see Sparks, the CRE's adjutant, and heard that the attack was expected on the 13th. Even as he spoke I could see batteries training – practising retirement – just outside.

Information became more definite. An attack at Bullecourt was expected on the 13th, and the big attack on our front on the 14th or 15th. We were ordered to take up ammunition to the positions reconnoitred for retreat – the 'Yellow Line' position west of Guyencourt. I stacked our ammunition in six great heaps, and reconnoitred the 'Yellow Line' OP. Returning I met a couple of tanks near divisional HQ, going up towards Saulcourt. They produced some surprise in me and much fear in my horse – a tall, half-trained bay, very nervous and given to getting up on his hind legs on the least provocation.

Slowly the days passed – the 13th, the 14th, the 15th – and the attack did not come. The strain was very great. Our plans were cut and dried, our defences were as complete as human will could make them. Behind the 'Blue Line' – the existing front line – and the 'Red Line' – which was the main line of resistance and included Epehy – were the 'Yellow Line', the 'Brown Line' and the 'Green Line' – five complete systems, comprising entanglements, posts, and trenches of varying depths – front lines, support lines, communication trenches, and all the other essentials of a defensive system. As far as organisation could make us, we were ready to meet the enemy's onslaught.

Still the attack did not come. At 2 a.m. on the 16th I left the railhead at Roisel, and, going by way of Havre, next day arrived at home.

Five days later the blow fell – the greatest blow ever dealt at any army in the history of war. On a front of 50 miles the enemy attacked – line after line of men, stretching for scores of miles in either direction, poured in upon our defences. Here and there our troops were overwhelmed by the flood. The 16th Division gave way, and early on 21 March the enemy were among the ruins of Sainte Émélie – the biggest sugar refinery in the world. Taking in front, flank and rear, the infantry of the 21st Division put up for a day and a half a fight which even the enemy described as 'bitter', and which, in the opinion of many, is worthy to rank among the finest in history.

On the right the line had broken. The Fifth Army was in full retreat. On the left, more slowly, the Third Army was withdrawing. The 21st Division did not withdraw: the two brigades in the line, the 62nd and the 110th, died to a man in defence of their positions.

The recapture of Sainte Émélie by the 11th Hants – pioneer battalion of the 16th Division – enabled the 21st Division Artillery to extricate itself, and to retire first to its prepared 'Yellow Line' positions and afterwards to its 'Green Line' positions at Driencourt and Aizecourt le Haut. On reaching the Guyencourt position, White found out that the enemy had mistaken my neat heaps of ammunition for guns in action, and had turned an 8-inch how battery on to them.

The retreat continued. There were not enough men to hold all the trench-lines which we had constructed, and the enemy had outflanked and crossed them on the right before our troops got back to them. Often there was no infantry between the guns, blocked in a long column of traffic, and the enemy. The 95th Brigade went back slowly but steadily by Haut Allaines, Manicourt, Bray and Dernancourt – familiar ground this – to Bresle. On the line of the Ancre, Villers Bretonneux, and the Avre, the enemy was successfully held, and his last big attack on 5 April was a failure. Amiens was held, the Channel ports were saved, and the British were not cut off from their allies.

I got back from leave on 1 April, but, like everyone else returning at this time, was detained at the base. I left Havre at 4 p.m. on 12 April, with Adam of C/95 and some 160 men of the 21st Divisional artillery, who had arrived from leave since the beginning of the offensive and had not been able to rejoin their units. Ignorant of our destination on starting, we proceeded via Amiens, where we were held up for some time owing to bombing by enemy aeroplanes, to Doullens. Here I found the 95th Brigade entraining for the north. I was too late to join my own battery but attached myself to B/95.

We left Doullens station about 8 p.m. on the 13th, and went through St Pol and Hazebrouck to a station near Poperinghe. As we left Hazebrouck guns were in action on both sides of the railway.

Arriving about dawn we detrained and were about to set out for Reminghelot, whither A/95 had already gone, when 'Taffy' Davies – 2nd CRA, 21st Division – rushed up and ordered us to proceed forthwith to Eeche and to take up a position of readiness north of the village. I followed the battery along the road in a civilian trap, the property of 2nd-Lt Roberts.

We found Eeche full of French troops and of refugees from the country to the south and east. The battery took up a position of observation near the village, and I stayed at the wagon-line, where I shaved, lunched, and awaited the arrival of 'A' battery from Reminghelot.

Major White arrived in advance of the battery with Baxter, and went forward to reconnoitre a position near Rouge Croix, on the Caister–Strazeale road. I followed later with the battery, which I picked up near Eeche church. In December 1915 Neale's battery had rested for a day or two at Eeche, and he had little difficulty in finding a wagon-line.

The gun-position, which was, in fact, situated some distance behind Rouge Croix, was in a double hedge. Farm buildings behind the position provided comfortable quarters for the officers and for the drivers and horse teams which remained close to the guns.

Having broken through the Portuguese front on 9 April and taken Armentières a day or two later, the enemy had possessed himself of a considerable tract of rich country, and his line now ran in a great arc from the Lys past Vieux Berquin to the La Bassée canal at Givenchy. We were on the northern face of the salient, and the enemy's line ran east and west through Menis, the Allies – English, Australian and French – being in Strazeele, Metereu and Bailleul. Our SOS lines lay in the square at Menis, and that evening White and I went up to the high ground east of Rouge Croix in order to register Menis church, but the light was too weak. In front of Rouge Croix we found a French officer sitting in a trench, laboriously acquainting himself with the country by means of a map cut from the *Daily Mail*.

The whole of my kit had been left at Longavesnes on 21 March, and had fallen into the hands of the enemy. Luckily I found stacks of abandoned blankets in what had been a gas school at Rouge Croix, and, having sent Thirlwell up for some of them, I spent the night in comfort.

The following is copied from a diary which I started keeping at this time:

15 April. Rouge Croix. This morning White and I went to Klein Hyl and to a farm on the ridge east of Strazele to find an OP. The Australians here appeared to think that the Hun was going back, and we saw some shells on Menis which White affirms were Bosch. Returned in time to show the general round the position. The new colonel seems nice [Col Sinclair was killed during the retreat from Epehy and Lt-Col Phillips MC was now OC 95th Brigade, RFA]. This evening went with White to reconnoitre a position north-west of Strazeele in case of further Bosch retirement. A thoroughly unattractive spot, but still.

16 April. Mont des Cats. Last night the enemy took Bailleul, and, fearful of a breakthrough, those in authority have rushed us up here. The colonel and I having reconnoitred a position for the battery north of Le Coq de Paille, I went to bring the battery up. Just as we were unlimbering the colonel rushed up and ordered us to proceed further east. After much difficulty, we found a bad position on the south side of the mountain, where we now are, and pitched a tent in a green field beside a stream. C/95 is just in front, and B is here somewhere too, as well as various batteries of the 116th Brigade. Nothing much is happening now, though everyone was retiring as fast as decency would permit when we came up this morning, and we saw one battery captain going down the road with his limbers at the gallop – saving the guns at Bailleul, a sort of VC stunt, I suppose.

17 April. Mont des Cats. We are still attached to the 133rd French Division, which has side-slipped to the left, and holds the line north of Metereu. Australian troops are on our right. This morning the major and I went forth to seek an OP from which we could see the Bailleul–Metereu road. We started towards the Quatre Fils Aymon but were deflected by a Bosch barrage and a French colonel, and eventually arrived at a place which we know as Goose Green, on the 'Quatre Fils' ridge, but north of the farm of that name. We got a good view of Bailleul, but saw nothing of Metereu and little of the road between them.

19 April. Mont des Cats. It has been snowing since 3 a.m., at which hour I was on duty during night firing.

20 April. Mont des Cats. There was snow on the ground this morning, but it soon melted, and the day has been fine. This afternoon Macdonell and I sallied out to find an OP. We climbed into a half-ruined barn at Quatre Fils Aymon, and got a fine view of Bailleul. But the position was dangerous, and Metereu – which is held by the Hun but almost surrounded by our line – invisible, so we left, and walked southward down the ridge towards Metereu. The road along the ridge was familiar – it was here that, before Loos, we got a wagon in the ditch, and Captain Park pulled it out for us. Though the road was swept at intervals by machine-gun fire, cows, pigs and hens abounded on it. In one farm we found a French battalion commander's servant busy milking a cow, in a shed with a dozen others. Returning, we eventually found a good OP behind a little mound on the hill north-east of Metereu. We do not seem to have a front line just here, and I really don't know if our mound is in No Man's Land or not. Having looked at the view and eaten some chocolate, we went back to the battery. Just before we got back it was heavily shelled, but we escaped without casualties, though 'B' and 'C' lost both men and horses. The gun-teams have now been moved back to a

safer spot – we do not want them quite so close now, as the Bosch seems to be held on this front.

The rest of our stay at Mont des Cats was uneventful. The weather was not good, but there was no more snow after 20 April. On our front the enemy made no further progress, but on our left he attacked repeatedly, and the drum-fire seemed continuous, often for days at a time. In this sector he captured Kemmel, but made no very great progress, and was heavily defeated by the 21st and other divisions when he attacked on the southern face of the Ypres salient on the 29th. Our infantry were holding Ridge Wood, and for the defence of this locality they received tanks from the Commander-in-Chief, by whom they were especially mentioned. They had already greatly distinguished themselves in this area when two brigades had been attached to the 9th Division and had recaptured positions on the Messines ridge.

A New Battery

Before we left our position I learned from White that I was about to be made captain of 'B' battery, in lieu of Ashdown, wounded at Epehy. I reported to Major Vyvyan-Pearse of B/95 RFA at his gun position south of the Mont des Cats after lunch on 1 May. I stayed at the guns for a day or two, during which the only event of note was the destruction of the mill on Mont des Cats by the Allies on 2 May, and then went down to take charge of the wagon-line.

I arrived at the wagon-line, which lay between Eeche and Godewaersvelde, on the 4th, after spending the morning at Godewaersvelde where a court-martial was sitting on Gunner Russell, formerly of C/96, C/97, and C/95. Early on the 5th we left Godewaersvelde and marched through Eeche, St Sylvestre Cappel and Cassel to St Momelin, north of St Omer. The guns remained in action until noon, and followed us to St Momelin. On the afternoon following we left this village and, marching through St Omer in the heaviest rain I have ever seen, arrived at [blank].

There we entrained, and, leaving at nightfall, arrived at Noyelles, near Abbeville, at dawn next day. We halted long enough to water, feed, and have breakfast, and then crawled on to Pontoise, where we repeated the process, with supper instead of breakfast. Another night on the train brought us on to St Gilles, and from there it was but a short way to Bouleuse, where we detrained. In all, we had spent about thirty-six hours in the train.

Leaving Bouleuse at about 11 a.m. on the 7th, we marched through Poilly, Sturey, Ville-en-Tardenoise, Romigny and Passy to St Gemme. This country north of the Marne was vastly different from Flanders. The trees were further advanced, and more like English trees. The villages were clean, and the rolling downs were as green as those of Picardy, but more wooded. The thin black-faced cows of Caestre were replaced by fat red-and-white ones. The whole landscape presented a picture of peace and plenty, very different from that which we had left. A tired division, we had come here for a rest, and here we seemed likely to find it.

The people all turned out to see us – we were almost the first British troops in this area, though I believe that the 8th and 50th Divisions were already in the line to the north of us. The people seemed very pleased to see us – at St Gemme we were billeted on the house of a refugee from Reims, an old lady who used to waltz round the table to the strains of the gramophone with Craig and Bostock.

Unfortunately the weather was bad and we were not in stables, so the position of the lines had to be frequently changed. This was the chief blot on a week of otherwise unsullied contentment.

After six days at St Gemme we packed up and marched through Bouleuse and Mery Premecy to Janvrey, where we spent one night in great comfort, thanks to the excellent arrangements of the French.

From Janvrey the Major, Adams and Bostock went on to the front to arrange about our relieving the 26th French Battery, which formed part of the artillery to be relieved by us – the 54th regiment. I brought the battery via Rosnay and Jonchery-sur-Vesle to Bouvancourt and we established a temporary wagon-line between the latter village and the hamlet of Vaux Varennes.

The guns went into action that evening and the next, four relieving the French in a position called 'Pantin', and two – the left section – going into an empty position known as 'Couteau'. Adams and Tomlin were at Couteau, Roberts and I at the wagon-line, and the remaining officers at Pantin.

The divisional front extended from the neighbourhood of Cauroy to the Aisne Canal east of Gernicourt, and was held by infantry in the following order from right to left – 64th, 110th, 62nd. These were covered only by the two divisional artillery brigades, the 95th being on the left, and B/95 on the left of the other batteries, on the edge of the 8th divisional area. On our left were the 8th Division, and beyond them the 50th Division. The three divisions above enumerated and, subsequently the 25th Division in reserve, formed the IX Corps, which was part of the Sixth French Army. They were all tired divisions sent here for a rest, and all had gained distinction during the past two months, the 21st and 25th having each been twice mentioned in official dispatches.

The sector, indeed was rather '*bon*', and we lived in great comfort at Vaux Varennes. We cleaned and disinfected the old French stables, and ultimately moved into them. The weather was fine and hot, and the men bathed in the stream. I was a sort of provision merchant for the mess – rather a job as canteen stocks were low. We were here in the wine country, and this, rather than whiskey, became our staple drink.

One afternoon much movement was observed behind the enemy's lines and during the night the battery fired some thirty rounds at communications. Except for this, they did no firing, and we had no difficulty in maintaining 400 rounds per gun at the positions.

In Retreat

Early on 26 May, as a result of a raid by our troops, we took one prisoner, and from him ascertained that the enemy would deliver a formidable attack at 3 a.m. on the 27th. This information did not percolate to the batteries till 9 p.m., or to the wagon-lines (officially) till 10 p.m. on the 26th. More diary extracts follow:

26 May. Vaux Varennes. Tonight we have had a great surprise. At 9.30 p.m. a heated officer rushed into the mess with the words 'The enemy is attacking at dawn – for God's sake give me a drink!' We gave him a little red wine, diluted, and he explained. As a result of the examination of a prisoner taken yesterday, who said that the enemy would attack at 3 a.m. tomorrow, the 25th Division had been rushed up from Fismes. He was the adjutant of the 112th Brigade RFA and was on his way to report to the CRA 21st Division. His HQ wagon-line was about to arrive at the camp, and his batteries would come into action during the night.

Soon a message from Brigade arrived, warning us to pack up and prepare to shift if a bombardment opens at 1 a.m., as this will herald an attack. I have warned the Battery Sergeant Major and, though I don't really believe that anything will happen, I have decided to start a diary. Everyone is most excited, but I do not expect to rise before 6 a.m., when I must get up to attend to a certificate for DADOS (Deputy Assistant Director of Ordnance Services).

27 May. Jonchery. At 1 a.m. today we were aroused by a terrific bombardment. Realising that the show had begun, we packed up and prepared to move. The Bosch fired many gas shells into our valley. In the middle of it a dazed veteran of the 8th

Division wandered into 'D' Bty's mess – he had lost his Small Box Respirator and his horse and everything else. Having been fitted up with a new Small Box Respirator by Bridge he departed. By 4 a.m. the bombardment – phosgene and mustard gas – ceased, and I was just going back to bed when a whole battalion of the 25th Division walked into the camp. I settled them in, shaved, breakfasted, and lay down.

At perhaps 8 a.m. we were ordered to send up our gun-teams, and I went up with ours – six gun-limbers, Sgt Neil, Cpl Willets, and four horses in a GS wagon – and put them in a wood about 500 yards behind the guns. Then I went up to Pantin and saw Pearce, and he ordered me to withdraw the two guns from Couteau, one of which had lost a wheel. I went up there and got No. 5 out, and sent it off under Sgt Leech to the wagon-line. It took me some time to get a new wheel on No. 6 and to get it out of its pit, but by about 12.30 p.m. it was clear of the position, and was proceeding under Bombardier Grove to the wagon-line. I had given Adams instructions to find a new position north-west of Vaux Varennes, and he and I followed the guns down the road. We went on about 500 yards, and were there met by an excited infantryman, who told us that the Huns were in the wood between us and the advanced wagon-line where the gun-teams were, blocking the way home. Disbelieving it, I nevertheless diverted the gun across country to the left, and myself proceeded with some caution towards the advanced wagon-line. The gun was sniped at, and dashed off up a woodland track at the canter. I attempted to rejoin my teams at the advanced wagon-line, but was fired on, and had to make a detour, crawling through the long grass, and when I reached the advanced wagon-line I found nothing there except 'A' sects' abandoned limber, whose wheel had been taken away for No. 6 gun.

Then I tried to get back to the guns at Pantin, and reached the edge of the wood. The Huns were along the roadside about 100 yards off, and some of our horses were standing about beyond them, grazing contentedly. None of our men were to be seen. Deeming it imprudent to go forward, I retired into the wood, where I found a rifle which I picked up, and, a little further, some small arms ammunition. As I went along I met a subaltern of the 110th Brigade RFA, and walked along the tramway with him, sniping Huns – or rather, at Huns – when opportunity offered. We could see men advancing from our wood – Pantin – towards Bouffignereux. Retiring steadily but cautiously, we reached some parties of the South Staffords and Wiltshires (25th Division) without incident. We could see other troops lining the road south-west of Bouffignereux, and I began to have grave doubts if even our first gun had got away. Deeming it our business to get such guns as remained into action as soon as possible, we continued our retirement as far as the road from Châlons le Vergeur to Guyencourt, where we parted, I towards Vaux Varennes, he in a more easterly direction.

I found the wagon-line tranquil. Adams and Craig were there, also Sgt Leech and his gun, Cpl Willetts, and the second gun's team and detachment. They all seemed surprised and pleased to see that I survived, and, while our only remaining gun got ready to go into action, I ate and drank. After a while Pearse arrived on my horse, also Roberts and Driver Gilbert. While they fed, we learned what had happened. While I was at Couteau they sent for the other teams, and Sgt Neil led them up past the wood. Huns in the wood sniped them as they went by, killing numerous men and horses, and wounding Sgt Neil. Cpl Willetts, Driver Nash, 'A' sect's team – which had not followed the others – and five of the eleven drivers of the other teams regained the wagon-line. The others are missing. The failure of the teams – other than one pair of wheelers – to reach the position woke them up to the fact that they were almost surrounded. An attempt was made to extricate one gun, but the horses were hit, and the major ordered the men to shift for themselves. He and Roberts narrowly avoided capture as they left the wood. Outside they found my horse loose on the road, and brought him in. At present Bostock and a score of men are missing.

During the afternoon Roberts and I got the remaining gun into action north-west of Vaux Varennes, and fired on the enemy approaching Bouffignereux and Guyencourt. On the right our line seems to have held, but on the left the enemy has got right through.

At 7 p.m. I returned to the wagon-line and prepared to move it. When I arrived it was gone, and it took us – Tomlin, Roberts and myself – a long time to find it. In the end we found them entering Jonchery: apparently the colonel packed them off without telling anyone. Tomlin went off with a couple of loads of ammunition for the gun, which is in action somewhere between Vadiville Farm and Pevy, and I brought the wagon-line on. I have planted it in a cornfield here: I hope we are out of it early tomorrow, in case some Assistant Provost Marshal comes along and sees us.

28 May. Mery Remecy. About 7 this morning Tomlin rushed in with the news that the Hun were upon us. As we got ready to move we heard machine guns very close. We left the place at top speed, but had calmed down a bit when we passed through Jonchery. As we entered the town, a major-general officer asked us whether there were any infantry the way we had come! The roads were crowded with refugees, and it was nearly 11 a.m. when we arrived at Treslon, where we pulled on to a bare field and prepared to settle down, only to receive orders to retire forthwith to Mery Remecy. We lunched and then got on the road again. At Poilly we passed a lot of wounded and French nurses, apparently waiting for a train. At Bouleuse scores of lorries laden with troops passed us, going north-east. In the end we fuelled at a big field here – a very pleasant place, except that there is a whole shed full of gun-cotton too close to be really comfortable. I left the

harness on till 8 p.m., and then took it off as there was no sign of approaching enemy. Our gun has been attached to 'A' battery, and two of our wagons are up there now with ammunition. The major is doing liaison at 62nd Infantry Brigade HQ.

29 May. Chaumuzy. Today we handed over our gun to 'A' battery, and we have been doing Brigade Ammunition Column for the 94th. I was ordered to report to Col Boyd, and did so about 8 a.m., since which time Roberts has been doing liaison with 62nd Infantry Brigade. I went up the Rosnay road with four wagons AX, part of which I gave to B/94 when they retired to a point about half a mile north of Mery Remecy, and dumped the rest for 'A' and 'C' Batteries. I saw Murray Lyon up there, with some very thin teams – our horses were much better than the 94th – also Padre Smith, with whom I lunched on bully beef and biscuits.

When we came away we brought a whole lot of wounded, whom we dumped at a hospital near Aubilly. We rejoined the battery at Chaumuzy Mill, where the major had already arrived and taken charge. The 19th Division is much in evidence here, and a whole lot of French batteries have gone up.

29 May. Vanciennes. This morning we withdrew from Chaumuzy to Maufaux, and this afternoon still further. Five hours marching in an endless crawling column brought us to Fleury. I found a wagon-line here, but the major halted only long enough for tea and then we came on across the Marne. The enemy has reached the river at Dormans, and possibly on the right as well, where the situation is obscure, so I think we did well to cross the river. I believe the guns are in action about Fleury, but we don't know anything definite. We are sleeping tonight in an old French stable, which is both smelly and draughty.

10 June. Vanciennes. Today we returned to the 50th Division the five old spring guns they brought us yesterday. We are supposed to receive in their stead six new recuperator guns, but

they haven't come yet. The weather is still fine: this afternoon went bathing in the Marne.

We were popular enough in Epernay – in fact an old man there told the major that we were perfectly splendid and, if it had not been for us, the French would long ago have been overcome – but the only shop in Vanciennes would have none of us. Possibly as a result of German propaganda, the natives apparently believed that we had let them through, whereas I think it is now generally admitted that the fault lay with the French 22nd Division, which was holding a very extensive front on the left of the 50th Division. The French division having broken, the enemy advanced eastward, rolling up successively our 50th and 8th Divisions, and was only checked by the 21st, which retired slowly in conformity with its flanks, ably supported by the 25th Division.

Everyone admits that the fighting retreat of the 21st Division, with its left in the air but its right constantly in touch with the French, was a very fine performance. In comparing our achievements with those of other divisions, however, it must be remembered that the main weight of the blow fell on the 50th Division, against which many tanks were used. This unfortunate division was completely overwhelmed in what is said to have been the heaviest artillery preparation ever put down. Practically none of the infantry got back: in one artillery brigade, of the gun-line personnel only one major and one gunner returned. Early in June it was reported that the division had only 1,500 men left. At the same time, after several days fighting, the 21st Division could put only 1,100 men in the line, organised as a '21st Independent Brigade' of four battalions, viz. the 14th Northumberland Fusiliers, 62nd Company Battalion, 64th Company Battalion and 110th Company Battalion. In addition there was the Divisional Artillery, some 300 men short, and the 21st Machine Gun Corps Battalion.

Last Days on the Marne

Our new guns arrived late on the 10th. The general, seeing them in the gun-park that day, ordered us into action forthwith, and so, leaving Vanciennes after lunch, we marched through Epernay to St Imoges, where were the wagon-lines of the batteries in action. I went on ahead and, assisted by Neale, selected a wagon-line under the trees close to the Pourey road. Two French batteries had horses in the same wood, but they left a day or two after we got in.

Two guns – those of the centre section – remained at the wagon-line. The others went up that night and relieved C/95 in action near Ecueil Farm. The major, Roberts and Moody attached from Trench Mortars since 3 June – were at the gun-line, and I was alone at the wagon-line. Adams had left us a day or two before and gone as captain to N94, and Tomlin was attached to 'A' battery. Craig was on Brigade HQ as orderly officer, but Elliott, whom he had replaced, had gone to 'A' battery, which had lost Brown and Baxter killed.

Our chief difficulty at St Imoges was water. Though we were very high, there was a large pond or small lake quite close, but we found it quicker to water at a smaller pond used also by A/94. This pond was hardly large enough to support two batteries, but by good fortune we had just enough rain to keep it going.

We were a very long way from the guns – it took wagons six hours to go there and back. The gun-teams remained in a wood behind the position under Sgt Tapner. Our village contained, in addition to our wagon-lines, a number of French troops, and the headquarters of the 3rd Italian Infantry Division, which had now taken over this part of the line.

Though I did not speak to any Italians, and did not know an officer when I saw one, what I saw of them impressed me favourably. Their transport, for instance, was far less 'rag-time', and their general bearing far more English, than that of the

THE OFFICERS,
N·C·Os, AND MEN OF OUR·BATTERY SEND YOU THEIR
Christmas Greetings

FROM THEIR LITTLE DUG-out in [deleted by the Censor]

On Xmas 1915.
On active Service.

32. Battery Christmas card, 1915: Meeres commented that the gun-pit at Armentières was very like this.

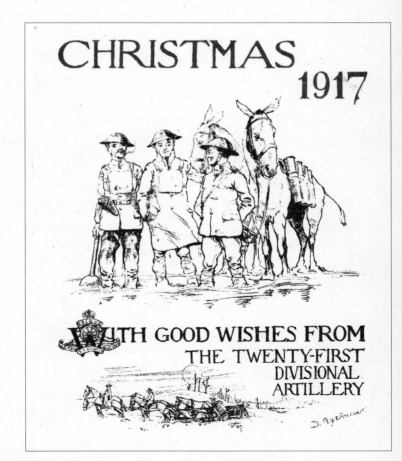

CHRISTMAS 1917

WITH GOOD WISHES FROM THE TWENTY-FIRST DIVISIONAL ARTILLERY

33. Divisional Christmas card, 1917.

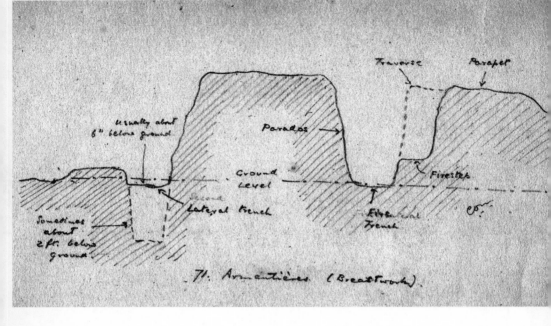

Usually about 6" below ground

Ground Level

Lateral trench

Sometimes about 2 ft. below ground

Parados

Traverse

Parapet

Firestep

Fire trench

71. Armentières (Breastwork)

Above, below & opposite top: 34, 35 & 36. Types of trench.

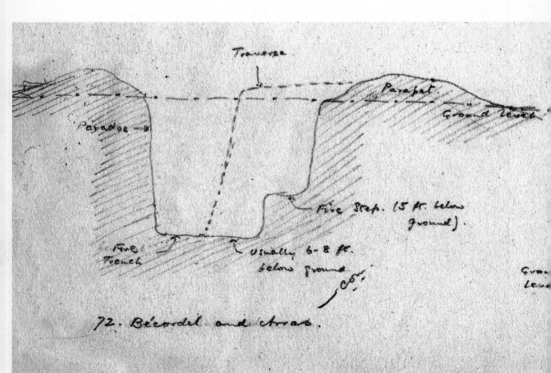

Traverse

Parados

Parapet

Ground Level

Fire Step. (5 ft. below ground).

Fire Trench

Usually 6-8 ft. below ground.

Ground Level

72. Bécordel and Arras.

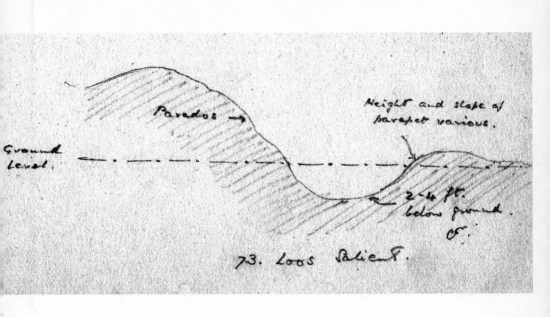

Ground Level

Paradox →

Height and slope of parapet various.

2-4 ft. below ground.

CF.

73. Loos Salient.

37. C/96 arriving at Havre.

23. C/96 arriving at Havre.
11·9·15.

1. Troops advancing to the Battle of Loos.
25-9-15.

Above: 38. Troops advancing to the Battle of Loos, 25 September 1915. *Below*: 39. Marching in Flanders. *Opposite*: 40. Farmers' Lane Tunnel, Loos Salient.

186. Marching in Flanders.
26-12-15.

484.

...ners' Lane Tunnel,
Loos Salient.

Above: 41. Trench 71. *Below*: 42. Grand Porte Egal.

Above: 43. Trench 69. *Below*: 44. Trench 70.

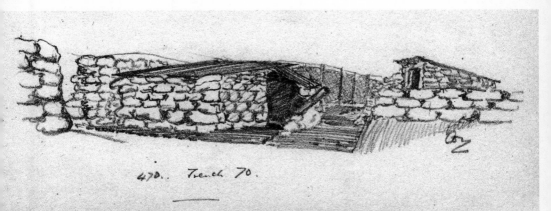

47b. Trench 70.

Above: 45. The Lens Road, 27 September 1915. *Below*: 46. Trench 70, Armentières.

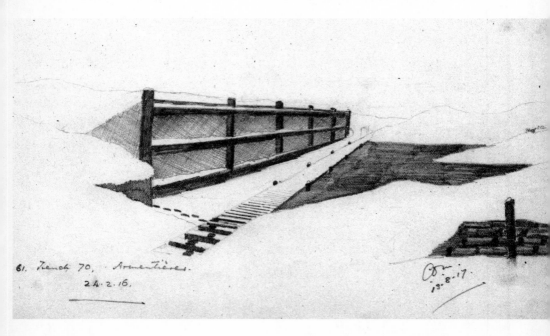

189. After a Bombardment.
19·1·16.

Above: 47. After a bombardment, Armentières, 19 January 1916. *Below*: 48. The raid on the Black Redoubt.

504. The Raid on the
Black Redoubt.

105. Preparing the Somme Offensive:
Ammunition Lorries.
June 1916.

Above: 49. Preparing the Somme offensive. *Below*: 50. Officers' mess, Becordel, June 1916.

201. Officers' Mess. Becordel.
June. 1916.

Above & Below: 51 & 52. A battalion headquarters, Becordel.

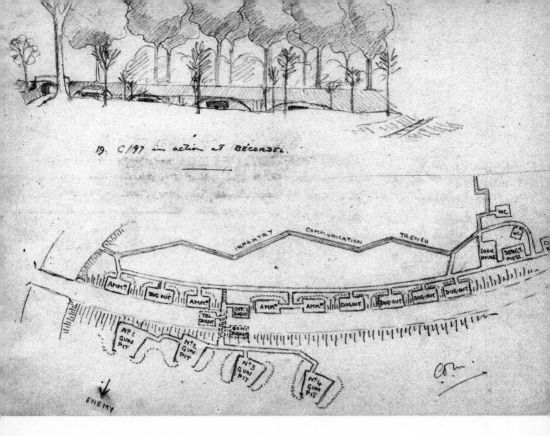

19. C/97 in action at BÉCORDEL.

Above: 53. C/97 in action at Becordel. *Below*: 54. The road to Fricourt.

205. The road to Fricourt.
14-9-16

Above: 55. Meaulte. *Below*: 56. At the wagon-line.

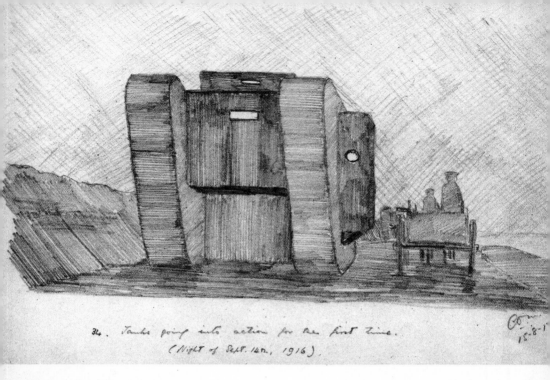

34. Tanks going into action for the first time.
(Night of Sept. 14th, 1916.)

571. The "Grand Stand", Fricourt.
April. 1916.

Above: 57. Tanks
going into action
for the first time.
Left: 58. The
'Grand Stand' at
Fricourt.

39. Flers.
17-9-16.

Above: 59. Flers,
17 September
1916. *Right*: 60.
A German dug-
out.

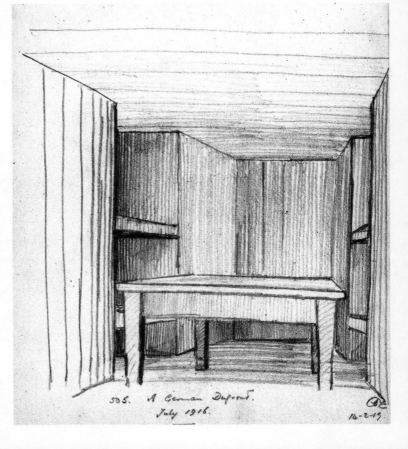

505. A German Dugout.
July 1916.

16-2-19.

29. *Mametz Wood* — 18.7.16.

Above: 61. Mametz Wood. *Below*: 62. High Wood.

Above: 63. A sniper's box in the trenches. *Below*: 64. A sentry.

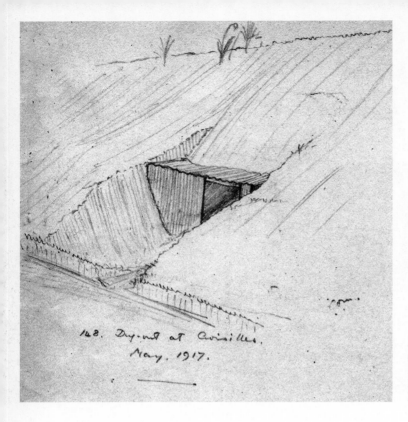

148. Dug-out at Croisilles.
May, 1917.

Left: 65. Dug-out
at Croisilles.
Below: 66.
Infantry Brigade
HQ.

149. Infantry Brigade H.Q.
May 1917.

Above: 67. St Michel-sur-Ternoise, 25 March 1917. *Below*: 68. Part of the 21st Divisional Rest Station.

93. Part of the 21st Divisional Rest Station.
23-6-17.

198. A Flemish Barn   26.3.18

Left: 69. A Flemish
barn.
Below: 70. Rowland's
Yard, Longavesnes.

197. Rowland's Yard, Longavesnes.
15.3.18.   25.3.18

Right: 71. St Gemme, May 1918. *Below*: 72. Retreating through Jonchery, 28 May 1918.

280 Retreating through Jonchery.
28·5·18.

347. Delivering ammunition.
17 - 9 - 18.

Below: 73. The Canal du Nord. *Above*: 74. Delivering ammunition.

242. The Canal du Nord – Feb. 1918.

Above: 75. Field-gun captured at Bois le Duc. *Below*: 76. My entry into Poix-du-Nord, 24 October 1918.

409. The K.O.Y.L.I. in Poix-du-Nord.
24-10-18.

77. The KOYLI in Poix-du-Nord, 24 October 1918.

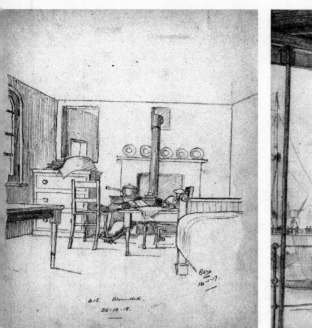

Above left: 78. Wounded, 24 October 1918. *Above right*: 79. Hospital ships at Havre.
Below: 80. The Western Front in the First World War.

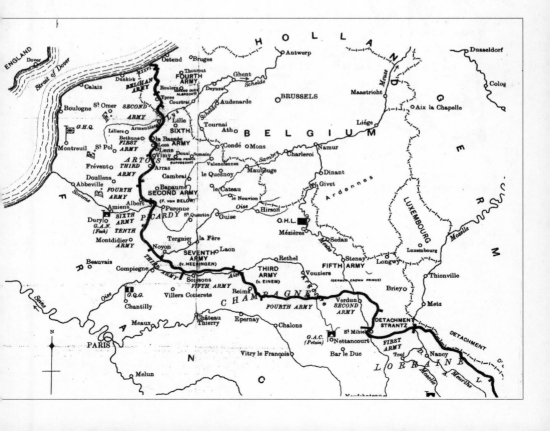

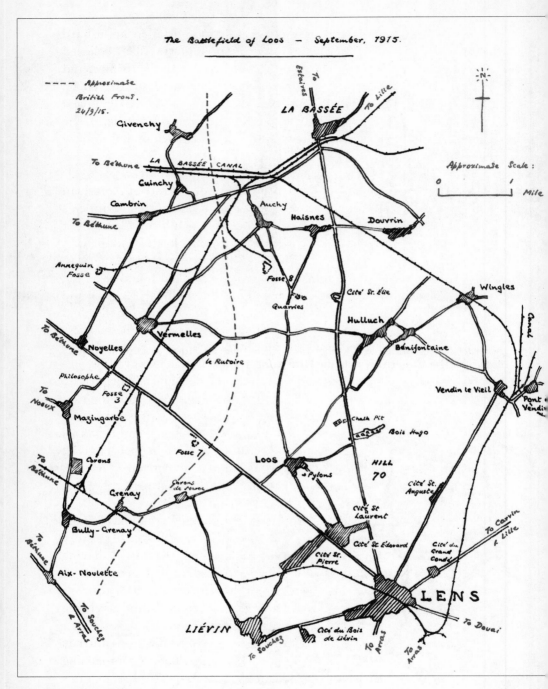

81. The Battle of Loos.

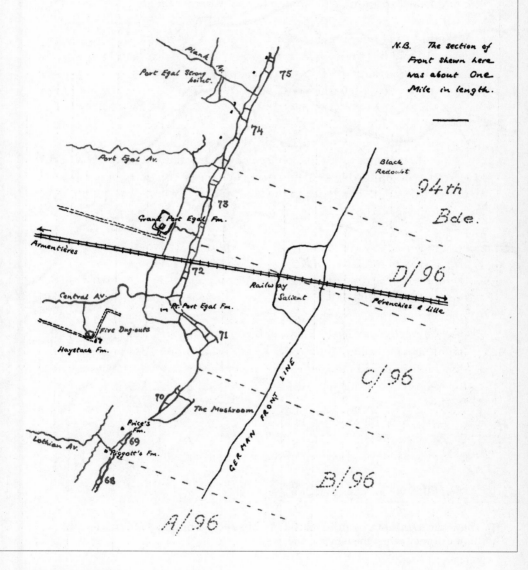

The British Positions astride the Armentières—Lille Railway,

October, 1915.

N.B. The section of Front shewn here was about One Mile in length.

Plank Tk.

Port Egal Strong Point.

75

74

Port Egal Av.

Black Redoubt

94th Bde.

73

Grand Port Egal Fm.

Armentières

72

D/96

Central Av.

Railway Salient

Pérenchies & Lille

Pt. Port Egal Fm.

Five Dug-outs

71

Haystack Fm.

C/96

70

The Mushroom

GERMAN FRONT LINE

Price's Fm.

Lothian Av.

69

B/96

Piggott's Fm.

68

A/96

82. Armentières.

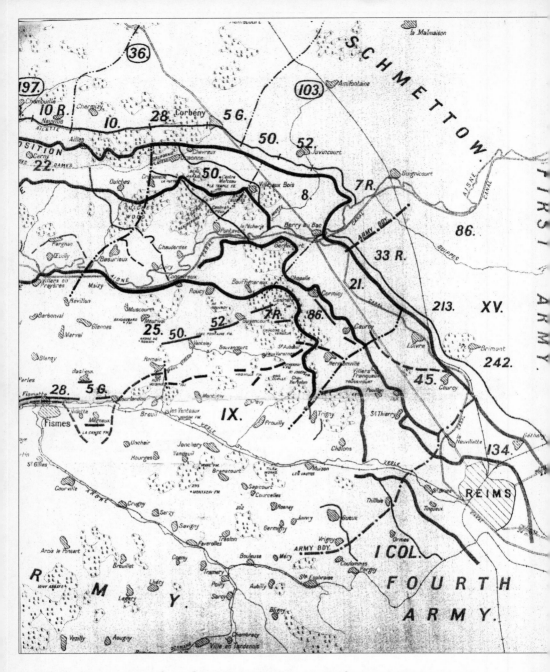

83. The German breakthrough, 27 May 1918: Meeres and his gun battery were just north of Cormicy when the attack came.

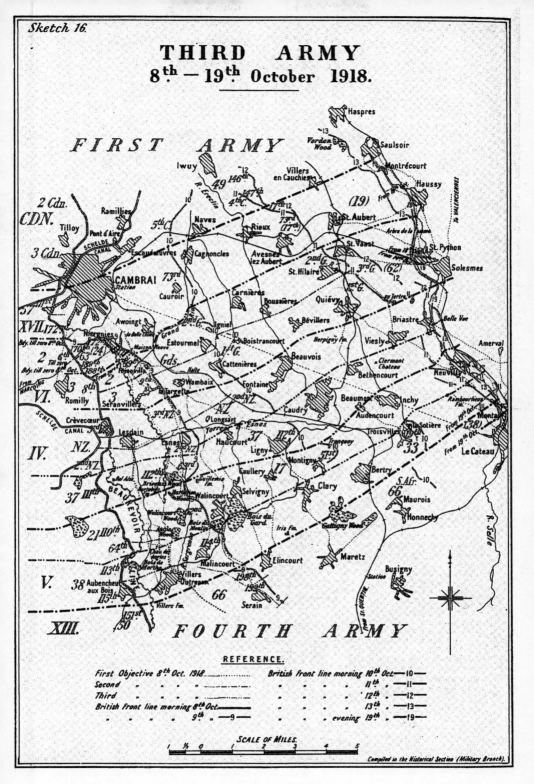

84. The Third Army, 8–19 October 1918: Meeres and the 21st Division advanced though Montigny, Inchy and Neuvilly.

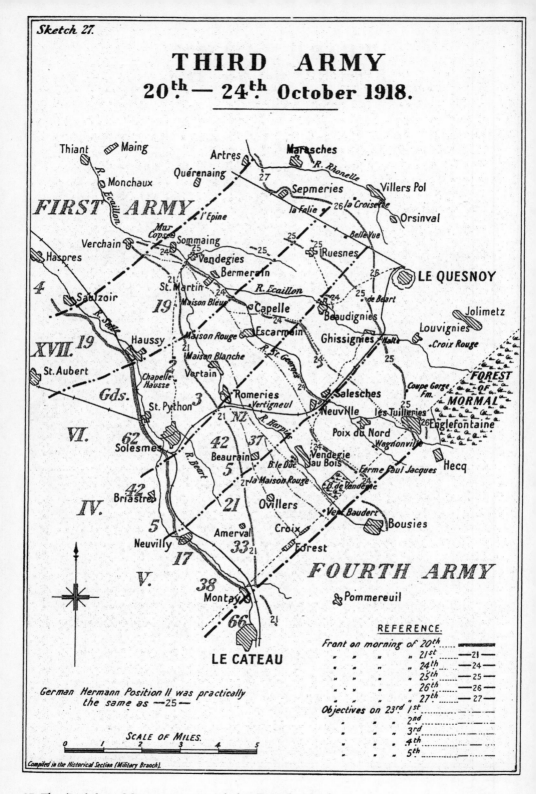

Sketch 27.

THIRD ARMY
20th — 24th October 1918.

Thiant · Maing · Artres · Maresches
R. Rhonelle
Monchaux · Quérenaing · 27 · Sepmeries · Villers Pol
FIRST ARMY · l'Epine · la Folie · 26 · la Croisette · Orsinval
Mur · Sommaing · Belle Vue
Verchain · Copse · 25 · Ruesnes · 26
Haspres · 24 · Vendegies · 25 · 25
4 · St. Martin · Bermerain · LE QUESNOY
19 · 21 · R. Ecaillon · 24 · 25 · de Beart · Jolimetz
Saulzoir · Maison Bleue · 24 · Capelle · 24 · Beaudignies · Louvignies
XVII. · 19 · Haussy · Maison Rouge · Escarmain · Ghissignies · Halt · Croix Rouge
St. Aubert · 21 · Maison Blanche · R. St. Georges · 25 · 25
Gds. · Chapelle · Vertain · 25 · 24 · Salesches · Coupe Gorge · **FOREST**
Hausse · St. Python · 3 · Romeries · Vertigneul · Neuvlle · les Tuilleries · 25 · **OF**
VI. · 21 · NZ · R. Harpies · Poix du Nord · Englefontaine · **MORMAL**
62 · 42 · 37 · 26
Solesmes · R. Beart · Beaurain · Vendegie · Wagnonville · Hecq
42 · 5 · B.le Duc · au Bois · Ferme Paul Jacques
Briastre · 21 · la Maison Rouge · B. de Vendegie
IV. · 21 · Ovillers · Vert Baudert · Bousies
5 · Amerval · Croix · Forest
Neuvilly · 33 · 21
17 · **FOURTH ARMY**
V. · 38 · Montay · Pommereuil
66 · 21
LE CATEAU

German Hermann Position II was practically
the same as —25—

SCALE OF MILES.
0   1   2   3   4   5

Compiled in the Historical Section (Military Branch).

REFERENCE.
Front on morning of 20th ———
"   "   "   21st ——21——
"   "   "   24th ——24——
"   "   "   25th ——25——
"   "   "   26th ——26——
"   "   "   27th ——27——
Objectives on 23rd 1st ············
"   "   "   2nd ············
"   "   "   3rd ············
"   "   "   4th ············
"   "   "   5th ············

85. The final days: Meeres was wounded at Poix-du-Nord.

French. For the latter I could find little use. I heard of no French troops putting up a fight in the retreat: as a matter of fact, of course, many of them must have fought well, but these did not appear to be in our sector. The French NCOs were polite and obliging, but the officers had no manners, and I did not meet a single one who would go at all out of his way to oblige an Ally.

On the evening of the 15th, the 94th having gone already, the battery was relieved by French troops attached to the Italians, and pulled out, arriving at the wagon-line at midnight. Next morning we all marched off, through Dizy-Magenta, Ay and Epernay – a circuitous route fixed by the French traffic control – to Voipreux, near Vertus. Military police belonging to the 19th Division – the only British troops remaining in the area – accompanied us to pick up stragglers, but had nothing to do.

Next day we marched to Normee. The people of this country appear to be thoroughly mean – claims poured in. On the 18th we marched to Sommesous and entrained, leaving the station on the 19th. We passed by Sens and up the valley of the Seine, round the west and south of Paris to Poutoise, and on through Sevifontaine to Lougpre, near Abbeville, where we alighted after some thirty hours in the train.

For breakfast we pulled into a field, where our presence was much resented by a bomb-fearing colonel of a neighbouring Casualty Clearing Section. If the authorities will put hospitals beside important railway junctions, how can they blame the enemy for bombing them? Having finished breakfast, we marched though Oisemont to Neslette.

Magrath – recently posted from N95 – had gone ahead as billeting officer, and he and Martin between them had fixed us up in the worst camp possible. The wagon-line stood on a chalk ridge, exposed to driving rain, and about fifteen minutes' walk from the officers' and men's billets, which were inadequate. Fortunately on this occasion we spent only two nights in this paradise: we came back to it later, but under better conditions.

On the 22nd, rising betimes, we marched through Blangy-sur-Bresle and Tacheville to Touffreville-sur-Eu. We shared the village with 'D' battery, the rest of the brigade being at Flogues, and headquarters at Mesnil-Val. The 94th was in Eu.

At Touffreville the men lived, as usual, in barns. The sergeants had a mess in a farm, and when they came down to breakfast their hostess – Mme Victoria Polly by name – would put a dozen fresh eggs and a great jug of milk on their table. But the officers were best off of all. We lived in a '*castelet*' belonging to M de Porte Riche, of the Grand Hotel, Biarritz. Each of us had his own bedroom with a gilt double bed. In addition there was a dining room, anteroom, billiard room and two trout streams. It was the best billet that I have ever had in France.

The sea was about 3 miles off. One day Tomlin and I took the whole battery to bathe in it at Criel-Plage. Criel, and especially Eu and Le Treport were the centres of life, but unfortunately only the first was accessible to the men.

While at Touffreville we received fifty-one men as reinforcements, including a number of sergeants and corporals. We also received some of our long-awaited stores, and, what with the six guns and thirty horses obtained at Vanciennes, we began to look quite like a battery again. At the same time 2nd-Lt T. Evans joined us from England.

The infantry who were near us in the Eu area were also receiving reinforcements, and, for the third time in three months, we found ourselves with battalions consisting almost entirely of recruits prepared like their predecessors to uphold and increase the fair fame of the 21st Division. Since 21 March the British Army had received a series of rude shocks. Its strength had been greatly diminished and, to make up other divisions, a number of those which had suffered most were split up, their staffs going back to England to bring out fresh divisions bearing the glorious old numbers. Our friends the 25th Division had formed one division with what remained of the 8th and 50th, the new unit bearing the old number of the 8th Division, and we were left with the honour of being the British division most often mentioned in the dispatches of the Commander-in-Chief.

[According to the *Official War History*, 95 Brigade brought back its barrage to protect the battle zone at 8 a.m. on 27 March. 95 Brigade, threatened by the enemy's advance, on the 8th Division front, was ordered to retire at 10 a.m. Before the order arrived the battery was surrounded by the enemy and only one gun out of the six was saved. The remainder of the brigade withdrew between 11 a.m. and 12:30 p.m., having to abandon two guns.]

Rest after Toil: the Influenza Pandemic

We were just beginning to make friends in Touffreville – in fact we had a whole French family in after dinner at the moment – when, at 10 p.m. on 29 June, we received an order warning us that we should probably move on the morrow.

Sure enough, we marched off early in the morning towards Martaineville. Brigade HQ had timed our march badly, and we were very late passing through Beauchamps. From there we went to Gamaches and – after losing ourselves once and having to reverse – to Vismes-au-Val. There we learned that we were miles away from our destination, which was our old haunt – Neslette. It had been changed after we started, but brigade had not thought it necessary to inform us. From Vismes-au-Val, I went on ahead and, arriving in Neslette at dusk, dined with 'A' battery. I saw nothing of Magrath, who was billeting officer: as a matter of fact, he was sleeping in the farm where we had messed last time. The battery got in at 11 p.m., and, expecting to go on next day, the major decided not to go into billets, but to sleep in the field.

As a matter of fact, we did not go on. The 'Spanish Influenza', which had claimed several victims – including all the officers of the battery except Tomlin and myself – at Touffreville, was now so prevalent as to make it apparent that, if ever we did arrive in the neighbourhood of the line, we should be left with too few men to go into action. We were expecting to go on the day after, but that also was cancelled.

And so on, each day. Men went sick at the rate of about eight per battery per diem. A camp was formed down by the river, and all the sick were thrust into it – not only those with influenza but all the ordinary daily casuals as well. It is not to be supposed that all who went down there were genuine cases: the temptation to bask by the river in the sunshine with absolutely nothing to do must have been strong enough to induce a certain skill in malingering in even the dullest of our usually hard-worked men. At any rate, the numbers in the camp grew so that the brigade was completely immobilised.

The disease originated, I believe, as far as we were concerned, in the Eu area. The infantry suffered as severely as we. The 94th Brigade got one stage further on its march, but then it, also, had so many sick that it could not go on. No. 1 section of the DAC had had ninety sick before ever they left the Touffreville area, and an officer No. 1 Company, 21st Divisional Train, told me one day that, if ten more of their drivers went down, they would be unable to send up rations.

Meanwhile the numbers in our camp were growing. Two parties of fifty went off to Mers to convalesce by the seaside. The second of these was under Magrath, who had been sick at Neslette.

We made spasmodic efforts to do some training, but achieved little, as we had so many men away, and got quite a good rest. We did a little gun-drill, and the battery staff went out once or twice, but that was all. Towards the end of our stay a number of sports meetings relieved the monotony, and afforded entertainment to the good people of Blangy, with whom we, and especially the DAC, were very popular.

At this time the Third Army was clamouring for us, but we sat still, having, as we affirmed, too many sick to permit of our moving. Much time was lost. Still, the rest was doubtless good for us, and was certainly earned, and the opportunity to get ourselves together was invaluable as we had so many reinforcements.

By 21 July the epidemic had almost worn itself out, and next day we left Neslette and marched via Oisemont to Lieracourt, some miles south-east of Abbeville. Billets were poor, except mine, which was excellent.

Next day we marched through Hicecourt and St Ouen to Havemas. We were leading battery, and took a wrong turning soon after starting, so the leading section – the right – had to reverse and take the rear. The billets at Havemas were pretty good. The name of the village is familiar to most gunner officers: Havemas was the seat of the Third Army Artillery School before it went to Hauteclogue.

On the 24th we marched through Naours –V Corps headquarters – to a sodden valley between Raincheval and Mavieux. It was a very wet march, and the swampy vale allotted to us as a wagon-line was far from inviting.

We stayed for a day or two in our valley, and it rained hard all the time. We had a tent in a wood where the sun could not penetrate at all. While we were there the last of the influenza patients came back to us. The same day we had to hand over one of our new recuperator guns to 'C' battery in exchange for an old tank-buffer gun – an operation which was only completed after much haggling, in which, supported by my two Quartermaster Sergeants, I came off best.

On the 26th we went up into action. Guided by a man from B/315, whom we were relieving, I took the guns of the right and left sections by way of Vauchelles, Louvencourt, and a very muddy cross-country track, up into action at Mailly Maillet. Next day the centre section went into action in a position some 700 yards in rear of that occupied by the other four guns. The idea was that these four guns, being surrounded by trenches, should, in case of an enemy breakthrough, be fought to the last, and when they finally had to be abandoned, the two guns in rear were to lay on them over open sights and to destroy them. This wonderful scheme was apparently the product of the fertile brain of one of those skilful generals who sit well back at Corps HQ and wins their battles there, for, as a matter of fact, a substantial crest in front of the two guns prevented them from either seeing or hitting those in front.

I remained at the wagon-line. We were to take over B/315's lines south of Vauchelles. When I went up to see them on the 27th I found the battery gone, and a few men left pulling down sheds etc. I took over the remains of the sheds and a quantity of very poor Royal Engineers material from the NCO in charge, put a guard over it, and went home. Next day, when we arrived on the scene with the teams, we found that they had come over in force, thrust aside my guard, and carried everything off. As a matter of fact, I believe they were entitled to do so. I reported the matter to the major, and he to those above him, and a row seemed imminent, but actually fizzled out.

At noon on the 29th I heard that my leave to Paris had been granted, and that I was to go with Martin that evening. We went to Doullens and prevailed on the Railway Transport Officer to let us go by passenger train the next morning, which got us into Paris that evening.

We stayed at the Hotel Edouard VII, and had a very pleasant, very expensive, but not very restful stay. The weather was good for the most part, but towards the end of our stay it became first showery and then wet. 'Bertha' shelled the city twice during my stay, but no shells landed within a mile, I should think, of where I was. Everyone I saw seemed to take it very calmly – but then, as I say, there was nothing anywhere near them.

Meanwhile the tide had turned. The last great German blow had been countered by the French, and their advance had become a retreat. The British troops in Champagne had upheld and increased the great reputation created for them in that theatre by the 21st Division. Elsewhere the British were quiescent, but at any moment we expected to hear of a big blow following on the enemy's withdrawal from the marshes of the Ancre.

7

THE ALLIED ADVANCE, SUMMER & AUTUMN 1918

The Enemy in Retreat

I returned from Paris on 7 August. All the way up I heard tales of a great battle impending, of guns pushed right up into the trenches at Villers Bretonneux, and of tanks and cavalry massing in the Amiens area. The cavalry which had been at St Ouen a fortnight before had gone.

At the same time the papers told us that the enemy had withdrawn from his positions about Dernancourt and Hamel across to the other side of the Ancre. British patrols had pushed into Albert, but the enemy still held the centre of the town in strength.

I spent three days at the gun-position having a look round. One day I went up to the OP – a concrete erection in Titan Avenue, commanding a view of Beaumont Hamel and the shell-pocked, trench-scarred downs to Irles and Miraumont. Behind Beaumont Hamel a big white cross and leaned sideways: it was one of hundreds which, collected in little white cemeteries or scattered broadcast over the historic battlefield, marked the resting-places of the heroes of the Somme and the Ancre.

On 13–14 August the enemy began to withdraw from his positions about Serre and Beaumont Hamel. Our infantry followed, but did not press him much, although they attempted to rush one or two machine-gun nests and suffered rather heavily in the process. The 95th Brigade advanced to positions on the road between Mailly Maillet and Auchonvillers, B/95 being in action just behind the light railway track.

For a day or two we had the limbers in an orchard at Bertrancourt, ready to go up and take the guns forward when required. Early on the 16th, however, they were withdrawn to the wagon-line, as the Bosch did not seem to be disposed to retire further, nor did we compel him to do so. It seemed that the excitement was over, and we settled down again to a peaceful routine. We even made a collection for the Royal Artillery Prisoners of War Fund, to which the battery subscribed more than 2,000 francs.

We had teams out night and day taking ammunition to the guns. They had one or two casualties at the position, and at least once the teams had to beat a hasty retreat. One of our horses was wounded in Mailly Maillet in taking up ammunition.

Then, very suddenly to us 'wagon-line wallahs', we assumed the offensive. Early on the 21st the Third Army threw itself against the enemy, on the whole front between Albert and Moyenville.

The following is my diary:

21 August. Serre Road. Last night, quite suddenly, we got orders to move. The gun-limbers – four of them – went up in the evening, and I took up twelve wagons – six of ours and six of Linsell's – after dark. We had to be at the 'Apple Trees' on the Serre road, outside Mailly Maillet, at 11.45 p.m. We arrived nearly an hour early, but soon after our arrival two of our guns passed on their way from Auchonvillers to the new position, and we hooked ourselves on behind and went with them.

They wanted eighteen loads of ammunition before dawn, so our teams had to do two trips, and got home very late. I was even later, as I called in at our old orchard at Bertrancourt and fixed up the limber-line there. In the end I got to bed at 5.30 a.m.

Nevertheless I was up in time for 9 a.m. parade this morning. More ammunition was called for, and I went out with the wagons at 11.30 a.m., thinking that I should be home early, and Tomlin could do the night stint. Well, we have taken twelve loads of ammunition up to the Beet Factory – they won't let us go up to the battery, because the road is under observation – and here we are in a field, and seem likely to stay here all night. So I seem to have got two nights out running.

22 August. Louvencourt. We stood to in our field till 7 p.m., the limbers joining us at 6 p.m. The major expected to advance, and so kept us handy – unfortunately we had nothing to eat – but, on learning that the battery would not move after all, he made us bring up eighteen loads of ammunition, and then sent us home. I got to bed at 2 a.m.

Today nothing much happened. Tomlin is up with ammunition. The wagon-line is to move early tomorrow, and I have been up to Bertrancourt to fix things up for a move to the orchard where Magrath has his limber-line.

23 August. Bertrancourt. We came here this morning, getting in about 9 a.m., and spent the morning fixing ourselves in. I was up at the guns this morning, but have got back quite early and look forward to a good night's rest. It's a pity we can't bring our house and beds from Louvancourt.

25 August. Miraumont. Yesterday we started to carry on with the usual routine. At 9 a.m. the Nos 1 received a lecture on 'turn-out'. But at lunch-time our troubles began.

We had to send up ammunition by daylight. I took the wagons to the dump to fill up, and Tomlin took them up. I got back from the dump to find that gun-limbers had been called for, and Magrath and his flock were just getting away. So, when all the rations and things had gone, I only had about three teams left in the wagon-line.

In the evening I went up with Bombardier Wilson to reconnoitre a wagon-line at Mailly Maillet, to which Craig was expecting us to go up next day. There I met Lodwick of the DAC, who said he had orders to deliver ammunition to the 95th Brigade wagon-lines at Miraumont that night. Supposing something to be wrong, I went in to see Diggle – DA was at Mailly Maillet – and told him all about it. He stamped and swore and tore his hair for ten minutes, and called the 95th Brigade all the unpleasant names he could think of for ten more, and then told me to gallop off to Bertrancourt and tell everyone to rush off to Miraumont.

I got to Bertrancourt in ten minutes, sent round to warn the other batteries – of whom 'D' had already gone – and started to pack up. We had only a few horses in, and no GS wagons, but got away alright all the same after much delay – I'm afraid Wescombe is not a very good Battery Sergeant Major.

Just outside the wagon-line I met Tomlin and Bombardier Gilbert – also Spot. They brought us along as far as Mailly Maillet, and Tomlin, who had just seen the major, gave me some idea of what was happening, and then went off home and (next morning) on leave. Bombardier Wilson and I went on ahead and eventually found the guns in action east of Grandcourt about 10.30 p.m.

Having dined, I went back to Beaucourt, whither Bombardier Gilbert and the sergeant major had brought the first-line wagons – the gun-limbers and firing-battery wagons were up with the guns – and installed them on a bit of shell-swept ground north-east of the village. Other batteries of the brigade joined us before dawn.

After a short, cold night I rose at dawn, watered, fed, and breakfasted, and went off to find out where the guns had got to.

They were directly under the GOC 110th Infantry Brigade, and expected to move as soon as it was light...

Across Old Battlefields
I continue my diary:

25 August. Miraumont (cont.). I found them gone, but Bombardier Cross was on the position, and directed me on. South of Miraumont I found 64th Infantry Brigade HQ, and saw Spicer of the King's Own Yorkshire Light Infantry (KOYLI) – our Epehy friend. Close by our teams were standing in a shell-pitted field. The battery was about 1,000 yards in front, in action on the road to Pys.

I went back to the wagon-line at Beaucourt, shaved, washed, and had a very poor thing in lunches, and then brought them on to Magrath's meadow. One GS wagon got overturned in a shell-hole, but otherwise we had no casualties. On arrival I sent off to Bertrancourt for sundry shelters and things: the wagon is not back yet.

Late this afternoon – during stables, when, for the first time that day, most of Magrath's teams had their harness off – the guns sent down a call for the 'whole show', and we took up gun-limbers and firing battery wagons. The major was forward somewhere, and Roberts was expecting to go forward at dusk.

After a bit the major got back. Apparently the idea had been that (our infantry having taken Gueudecourt – an old acquaintance) we should pounce into action at Ligny Thilloy, with the cavalry and armoured cars. The major had seen the cavalry go up – one troop of North Irish Horse on bicycles.

The infantry seem to have done very well, but they have not taken Gueudecourt. They took Le Sars this morning, and went on to a line running more or less north and south through Ligny Thilloy. In fact, our intended position remains in the hands of the Hun. So the left and right sections are 'resting' tonight at the old position, preparing to face the strenuous horse-artillery warfare which they seem to expect. I don't. The right section, meanwhile, is down here, having come out of action.

I have my sleeping-bag now, so expect to be warmer tonight. I am sleeping under a sheet strung on the pole of the water cart.

26 August. Miraumont. Still here. Last night I got very wet. When the rain was at its worst, the wind got up and blew away my sheet. After some delay I retrieved it and secured it with a safety-pin, exposing as little as I could of my person to the inclement weather but, nevertheless, getting very wet.

Late this morning, after rather a '*bon*' breakfast, I went off to seek the guns, and found them waiting at their rendezvous – a valley this side of the Serre. While I was there Miles received a note from the major, who was up with 62nd Infantry Brigade HQ, saying that we were still where we started from – i.e. about Ligny Thilloy – and that the battery was unlikely to come into action for some time. However, the teams were to stand to, and could not go off to Pys for water.

We had lunch in a valley off the road. He put a few shells round about, and a lot in Le Sars. He had left one or two little mines in the village: several have gone up today, causing casualties. On my way back here I met Holman, who said there was a water point at Le Sars. I hope there is: water is very scarce in the country in front of us, and the problem of finding enough for so many horses and men is a hard one.

27 August. Miraumont. Had a more comfortable night last night. Went up to the guns today, and found them in action just in rear of the forward wagon-line, which has not moved. After lunch I went up to the OP, which is on the Butte de Warlencourt. There was nothing much to see.

This evening I sent up teams to relieve those in the forward wagon-line – none too soon, I believe, as I hear that the horses there have had no water except from shell-holes, and that they would not drink.

I saw Craig this evening. He tells me that we hold Herleville, Montauban, Bazentin le Petit, part of High Wood, Luisenhof Farm, and part of La Barque. On the left we have taken Monchy-le-Preux and Fontaine-lès-Croisilles, and got through the Hindenburg Line. It must be fifteen months since we first attacked Fontaine: this is the first time we have got into it – it is our 'furthest east' in this area. It is reported that we have taken 42,000 prisoners in this show – the V Corps took twenty-three officers and 950 Officers of Regiment in twenty-three hours.

28 August. Miraumont. The war is becoming quite a fixture again. There is much firing going on now, and Craig seems to think that I shall have to send some ammunition up – I took up 400 rounds yesterday and they have only four guns in action. Magrath slept here last night, and went on leave this morning. He rode to Arleux or somewhere and, as usual, sent his horse back with a great sore on his withers. It has been wet all day and I have been at the wagon-line.

29 August. Miraumont. I took up a lot of ammunition today and, being by myself, tried to find a new way home. I got absolutely lost and finished up in Irles.

No sooner, apparently, had the batteries got a lot of ammunition dumped than they received orders to advance. The first news I got of it was at lunch-time, when a man came down with the major's horse which had jumped on a bayonet. I sent up Tomlin's horse for him, and followed at leisure myself. I found the battery in action at the south-west corner of La Barque. Miles had an order to the effect that wagon-lines were not to go north of Aqueduct Road, and, on my way home, I reconnoitred the country south of the road, which proved to be a particularly arid and uninviting tract. However, there is a small pond in Le Sars, and I shall move either there or to the valley east of Pys early tomorrow.

We have captured Bapaume and, judging from the position of the balloons, must have made a big advance in the south as well.

30 August. Le Sars. I rose very early this morning, and went to Pys to look round for a suitable wagon-line. The whole country is a mass of shell-holes – nowhere is there a patch of firm ground big enough to accommodate an ammunition wagon. This, and the fact that the pond is almost dry, compelled me to abandon the Pys idea and come here – M15 d 5.9, west of Le Sars and south of Aqueduct Road – instead. D/95, the 21st Trench Mortar Brigade – whose total transport is eight mules and eleven small arms ammunition carts – A/94 and C/94 are my neighbours. I saw Driver Lawlor this morning – I did not know he was still with the division – and several more of the old C/96 drivers. There seem to be more of them in C/94 than in C/95, where only about six remain of the sixty men I took there in 1916.

So far we have managed our watering all right. The pond at Le Sars will soon be drunk dry, but they are busy putting up troughs at the Butte.

This evening twenty men and thirty horses of the DAC attached themselves to me. I was up at the guns tonight, and saw Bailie-Watson, just returned to 'C' battery. He was on his way back from the OP, and told me that the Bosch was still in Riencourt – attacked this morning by the people on our left – but was blowing up dumps, etc. – a usual sign of retirement. Miles tells me that we have taken Vis-en-Artois. The idea seems to be that, as soon as the Bosch walks out of Beaulencourt, we shall walk in. The 17th Division will then pass through ours and carry on the good work, and we shall go into Corps Reserve at Le Tansloy. I suppose someone will have taken it by then.

31 August. Le Sars. Today the war has proceeded quietly. The DAC refused to deliver 'ammo' to me last night, and I wrote a very fierce report to the major today, but, on reflection, decided that their attitude was justified, and tore it up.

This afternoon the major suddenly demanded two guns and 950 rounds of shrapnel at once. I managed it alright, but had to turn out all my teams but two – one of F's whose horses are too thin to exhibit on the roads, and one of B's which overturns a wagon whenever it is asked to pull one. The column's four-horse teams got into difficulties among the shell-holes, and I think Lodwick will make them up to six horses.

Last night they dropped a few shells round the wagon-lines. Bosch aeroplanes circled overhead, but dropped nothing. I hope we shall have peace tonight. They have been putting gas-shells over by Pys all day.

1 September. La Barque. This evening I have moved in here, the battery having gone forward to Luisenhof Farm. I am not sure that it was very prudent: they have just dropped five bombs outside my tent, and the air seems full of shells. No casualties have yet been reported, and we will hope for the best. Still, I'm afraid we are in for a bad night.

2 September. La Barque. This place is much pleasanter by day. I have put the horses on the hill for tonight, and the men have dug themselves in a bit. Miles has come down, Moody having rejoined the battery, and tonight we are sleeping in a 'blinkstation' – a lamp signal station, I imagine – a '*bon*' little house on top of a hill.

The battery is still at Luisenhof Farm, but, being no longer within range of the Hun, expects to move. The division took Beaulencourt this morning.

3 September. Today the 42nd Division took Villers-au-Flos, we took Lubda Copse and the sugar factory, and the 17th Division took Le Transloy. The 42nd and 17th have met, are out of it for a bit. We have been expecting to come out for some days, but nothing is certain.

The battery went yesterday to Beaulencourt and came into action east of the village, but did not fire. I went up there this morning, and found them advancing again. Evans took the guns to a point east of the village, where we met the major and took up a position of readiness – or is it observation? – limbered up, poles down.

They expected to go into action at any moment, and Miles and I reconnoitred Villers-au-Flos for a wagon-line. However, I have not moved, largely because I found some more baths in the village and am bathing all the men – or would be, if the water arrangements had not broken down owing to the guns retaining the water cart – and issuing them with clean clothing. Miles and I bathed in the last of the water – we each had 1½ inches of thick, black, tepid liquid in the bottom of a round-bottomed cauldron where we could only balance with difficulty.

That ended the first stage of the advance. 3 September found us out of the line, in reserve behind the 17th Division. The enemy had ceased to resist, and was going back fast – so fast, indeed, that the 17th Division had quite lost touch with him.

In the Devastated Area

I resume my diary under date 4 September: Le Transloy. This afternoon the battery harnessed up and dashed off to Rocquigny. I was up at the guns when they received the order, having just taken a walk round Beaulencourt with the major, and found nothing of interest. The wagon-lines were to come to Le Transloy, and I came along and found a good place here. Then I went back and got the battery from La Barque, and by the time we got up here I found that a heavy battery had also pitched on my spot, and, unfortunately, had arrived first. I therefore came to this place, which, I find has a well and a pond of its own – no inconsiderable advantages, considering that all the water has to be brought up to the two official water-points in the village by lorry. Unfortunately, we are rather close to the main road, and smothered in dust – a very dry, odorous, suffocating dust too. I hope it will rain tonight, to keep it down. Two dead Huns mark our gateway: we must bury them tomorrow.

This evening I set off to pinch a water cart. Unfortunately the tank was not fixed to the carriage and, as soon as the shafts were raised, it slid off and spilt its contents – it was full – on the ground. The splash brought out in wrath a heavy major, its owner. What he said to Bombardier Clark I have yet to learn: these majors are fiery people.

5 September. Le Transloy. A recent General Routine Order fixed the jam ration at 2 ounces instead of 3 ounces per man. For the last two days we have had only 1 ounce, and today we have none. Nor do we seem to be getting the extra oats ration promised. Still, on the whole, we have done very well for food all the time, and I have also managed to keep the battery in cigarettes.

The watering difficulty is becoming very acute. Here, in the desert of the old Somme battlefield, there is no running water. Here and there we find a filthy pond, which the horses will not look at, and here and there a smashed-in well. Neither pond nor well here has been of use, and we have been watering from shell-holes, and praying each night for rain to fill them up for the morrow.

The battery is now in action at Rocquigny. I went up with ammunition early this morning. However they expect to sidestep to the right, as the 38th Division is going out. They have been held up on the Canal du Nord, and apparently it needs the 21st to force a passage.

During the morning I took eight teams off to the Luisenhof Farm position and one to the Beaulencourt position, and brought away all the ammunition left there – also a pair of wheels for the water cart which we are making for the advanced wagon-line.

6 September. Sailly-Saillisel. Late last night I received a couple of messages from the guns. I was about to destroy the envelope this morning, when I observed some writing on it, and this turned out to be the only important part of the show. The battery had relieved B/122 east of Saillisel, and the wagon-lines were to

change over today. Miles went to look at this place, which was near Morval, and returned with a most unfavourable report, so I decided to come in here instead. Driver Benson got his wagon stuck in the muddy bottom of a very deep shell-hole, and it took the whole battery two good hours to get it out: otherwise we got in without incident. The village is absolutely flattened, and a mess of shell-holes. There is no smooth ground big enough for a horse – let alone a wagon – to stand on. However, we got in somehow, and are fairly comfortable, as the horses are under one bank and the men have dug themselves into another, and there is a pond and lots of shell-holes full of water.

This evening I went up to the guns, but found them gone. In the end we found them in action a mile east of Manancourt. The forward wagon-line is somewhere along the canal but, though I searched for some time, I could not find it. All the same, I intend to move the wagon-line up early tomorrow to join it. The general was right and I was wrong: there's plenty of water in the canal. That's why I'm rushing up there as soon as I can.

7 September. Canal du Nord. We came up here this morning, leaving Sailly-Saillisel at 7.30 a.m. Just as it was passing one of our DAC wagons, a motor-lorry trod on a bomb, which went off, wounding one DAC driver and one mule. The mule remains at duty: the man was hit in the face and has gone off in an ambulance.

The road lay over a bare hillside, exposed to the view of several Bosch battalions and – according to Miles – to Revlon Ridge, which he holds – or held this morning. We got down safely, but he must have seen us pull into our wagon-line, as he put a few rounds into it with a 5.9 high-velocity gun. He got very close, but did no damage – we are well sheltered by banks. We are near the spot formerly occupied by the former wagon-line, which moved on before we got here. The guns are at Sorel, expecting to go on tomorrow, and the forward wagon-line is a mile behind them – a spot of Roberts' choosing, miles from any water. All the water for their horses has to go up by water cart from here, and, after two days up there, the horses have to come down here for four days and drink as much canal water as they can, ready for their next two-day waterless spell.

We are very comfortable here: it is a great change to be out of the Somme desert. Here, of course, the villages are mined, and always present is the smell of death, but otherwise the scene is very peaceful – though shells are frequent. I hope we'll have no bombs tonight: we are rather too near a bridge for safety.

8 September. Canal du Nord. We have had rather a busy day clearing old positions of ammunition, etc., and carrying out the necessary reliefs of the team at the advanced wagon-line, which remains still in its waterless copse. The guns have shifted to Neudecourt – to 'Barret's Valley', the starting point of my 4-mile march by the pole-star one night last winter.

I was at the guns today, intending to go up to the OP and look at Peiziere and Epehy and the old haunts. But it was raining, and blowing hard, and the major was thinking more of holding the roof on to the mess than of making war. They were shooting on Vaucelette Farm this morning, and the infantry were to take Peiziere and Squash Trench – our old support line astride of Andrew Street.

We have been neither bombed nor shelled since yesterday morning, though Manancourt has received a good bit of attention.

9 September. Canal du Nord. I am alone this evening. Miles has gone up to the guns, to his no small content. The rain is beating against the tent, and the wind is driving the green water in foam-crested wavelets against my door-step. The weather seems definitely to have changed for the worse, and the autumn to have set in.

Our advance is pausing. Today we attacked Chapel Hill, and got on to it, but I hear that we have been unable to hold it owing to the people on the right failing at Epehy. Further to the right we have recaptured most of the old haunts – Templeux-la-Forse, Tincourt, Longavesnes, Lieramont.

The Passage of the Selle

We spent one night at Caullery. Just before lunch on the 10th [of October], we received orders to march at once to Montigny. So, taking our half-cooked meal with us, we set out, Tomlin going ahead to find us a nice field and a house suitable for the officers. We did not expect to come into action at Montigny, though we did not know exactly how far the enemy had retired.

On the previous day, when the infantry of the 17th Division had relieved that of the 21st – or rather, had passed through it – the 21st Division Artillery HQ staff had also fallen back, and we were now under the 17th Division Artillery HQ. This arrangement became habitual. The 78th and 79th Brigades (17th Division), and our own 94th and 95th Brigades remained always in the line, while the infantry of the two divisions took turns to carry on the attack on the left sector of the V Corps front, and we came under the orders of the Divisional Artillery staff of whichever division had its infantry in front of us at the time. On our right the 33rd and 38th Divisions worked together in the same way.

Now that the 17th Division was in front of us, then, we were under the orders of the 17th Division Artillery HQ staff, and were acting only as reinforcement artillery, the 78th and 79th Brigades having to do the bulk of the work of supporting the advancing infantry.

We pulled into a field at Montigny about noon, and I went up to the house which was to serve as Brigade HQ to find out what to do. After a while the colonel arrived, much agitated. It appeared that we were to go into action at once. The enemy had rallied behind the Selle, a little river which ran in a north-westerly direction from Le Cateau, and his artillery would not allow our infantry to show their noses over the ridge on this side of the river. The 17th Division intended to seize Neuvilly – a village on the east bank of the Selle, some miles from Montigny – at 5 p.m. that day, and so to force the passage of the river before the enemy should have time to organise his defence. It was essential that we should be in action by that time, as the infantry could not hope to cross the ridge and advance over the open slope to Neuvilly unless we put down a heavy barrage on the village and on the enemy's observation posts on the hill beyond it. As we had no very great concentration of artillery, and could not put up a shrapnel barrage thick enough to screen the movements of our infantry, smoke-shell would be used, and of these I had a few and 'C' battery some more – the other three brigades being destitute of any.

As soon as I had received the barrage orders and a 1:20,000 map of the Selle valley about Neuvilly, I galloped off to the battery, and issued immediate orders for an advance. I decided to take Evans as regimental officer and to leave Tomlin to guide the battery. I cannot remember what Miles was doing. Probably he was either feverishly searching for our rations – Miles had a peculiar for mislaying the rations – or looking for a suitable wagon-line – the normal duty of the battery captain in moving warfare. For to moving warfare we came on this day – the only day's moving warfare in which I had indulged in three years' soldiering in France, and not a very '*mouvemente*' form even then.

I had received orders to go into action between Troisvilles and the Inchy–Le Cateau road. It was customary for the brigade to be allotted by Divisional Artillery HQ an area in which his batteries were to come into action. Sometimes this area was a large one as on 8 October around Malassise Farm, and on the 9th, north and west of Walincourt: sometimes it was only a short length of valley, as in this case.

Ordering Tomlin to bring the battery at a walk by roads which I showed him on the map to the bridge by which the Troisvilles–Inchy road crossed the ditch running down the centre of the valley, I set out with Evans, a director-man and a couple of signallers, with horse-holders, and rode across country to Troisvilles. The country was cultivated and the going was very heavy, but we arrived in good time, and I selected a position on the west side of the valley, north-west of Troisvilles, our line of fire to Neuvilly church passing almost exactly over the 'sucrevie' on the Le Cateau road.

The battery also arrived in good time, although the roads were blocked with traffic. Leaving Evans to get the guns into position in the places which I had selected for them, and Miles to get some more ammunition up, I went off to the ridge overlooking Neuvilly, accompanied by a couple of signallers laying a wire. I did not realize for the moment that this was the ridge over which no infantryman dared to show his nose, and that I was in front of our most advanced line of outposts, which lay just behind the crest. So I sat calmly down on the hilltop, registering the guns on some big wooden sheds on the hill behind Neuvilly and firing a few smoke shell to determine the direction and strength of the wind. Between times I turned feverishly to my map, orders, and note-book, and hastily worked out the barrage. I got it worked out – it was not a very 'curly' one – and the guns received their orders for the opening line and range at 4.53 p.m.

So far the enemy had not disturbed me: I can only suppose that the failing light had saved me. About 4.55 the attacking infantry began to come over the hill past me in small groups – 'artillery formation'. At 4.58 Evans arrived at the OP. At 5 o'clock precisely the barrage opened – a continuous curtain of white shrapnel bursts stretching along the valley as far as the eye could see in either direction. At 5.10 the enemy opened a counter-barrage on the crest where we sat.

By this time the infantry were going down towards Neuvilly. The enemy's barrage on the crest did not catch them: no doubt, however, it would catch the second attacking line. 'Whizz-bangs' and bigger shells burst all round us. Our telephone line was soon cut in many places, and, after a while, seeing that it was impossible to restore communication with the battery, we returned thither, our retirement over the broad back of the hill being, to say the least of it, exciting. How it was that all four of us escaped, I do not know.

Having descended out of the deafening clamour of the barrage and made our way along the valley past rows of guns, all firing, we arrived at the battery position. I had intended to direct the smoke-screen myself from the ridge, but the cutting of our telephone had rendered this impossible, and in the end we did not fire our smoke shell till halfway through the barrage. Perhaps, as it turned out, this was as well, as we put up our screen after 'C' battery had used up all their smoke ammunition, instead of merely thickening their curtain as we should have done if we had fired it earlier.

It was dark before the barrage ended. Going forward beneath it, the infantry, on approaching the Selle, had been met with such a torrent of machine-gun fire that they could make no further progress. The attack came to a standstill. To our right our line had been advanced as far as the river. In the centre the enemy still held Neuvilly, including the smaller portion on the south-west (or near) side of the stream, and our line of outposts bent back round it. On the left we held the line of the road, parallel to and some hundreds of yards west of, the river. In no place had the river been crossed.

We received high praise for that day's work. We had been the first battery in the divisional artillery in action at Troisvilles: we had been the only battery accurately registered in time for the barrage: and we had been the only battery with enough ammunition at the guns to keep up the rate of fire ordered all the time. It had required much organisation on the part of Miles and myself to get that ammunition up in time, but the apparently impossible had been achieved, due principally to his efforts. The colonel was extremely pleased with us: for once he and his brigade had secured a distinct victory over the wily Boyd and the 94th. From that time on he treated me with much respect, and deferred to my opinions as though I was the most experienced of majors!

We slept that night in a shallow hole in the ground at the foot of a small bank, covered with a 'gun-cover'. The night passed quietly. We slept confident of work well done. How different from the night of that same day three years before, when I slept in the trenches as the representative at Battalion HQ of Keate, who had just killed some of our own infantry! I did not however realise that night that it was the anniversary of that unfortunate occurrence.

We remained at Troisvilles for some days, enjoying ourselves considerably, though for the most part the weather was very bad, being very wet, though warm. Troisvilles had been heavily shelled on the 10th, but afterwards was left alone for some days. There were civilians in it, the other three batteries had messes in it, and Brigade HQ and a heavy battery's wagon-line lived on the north edge.

There also Tomlin and Evans rigged up a bath-house, and all the officers and the gun-line personnel revelled in hot baths – in most cases the first since La Barque. Further, being among cabbage-fields which no one owned – the majority of the civilians having been deported by the enemy – we had green vegetables with our meals every day.

But all this time we were not idle. Renewed efforts were made to take Neuvilly. On the 11th, towards evening, Tomlin and I trudged down over the wet fields to one of our posts at the mouth of the ravine facing Neuvilly. From some officers half way down the ravine we learned that an attempt was to be made that evening to 'pinch out' the village. Advancing silently, without artillery preparation – no longer a necessity, as the zone of barbed-wire entanglements had been left far behind us – our infantry was to cross the Selle on both sides of the village and join up behind it. Surrounded, the German garrison would have to surrender. It was the plan which had succeeded at Fricourt two years before. The attempt, however, failed. I do not know why. Possibly it was made with inadequate forces – our old fault at Croisilles and at many other places – possibly it was never made at all. At any rate, no ground was gained.

Next morning, however, another attack was made, the general idea being the same. Advancing by a barrage put down by (I think) five brigades of artillery, one brigade of infantry was to cross the bridge on either side of Neuvilly, the village was to be 'pinched out', and our troops were to go right forward and seize the high ground beyond.

The barrage was put down, and after it, having shaved and breakfasted, I went up to our OP, which was established in an old shell-hole on the ridge – possibly one of those made on the day when we were so heavily shelled up there. The weather being thick, I could see nothing of the situation, and decided to go forward and investigate. Evans volunteered to go with me and, and accompanied by him and by one signaller, and armed to the teeth, I set out to seek the front line.

Descending the ravine, we debouched on the flat land south of Neuvilly and gained without difficulty the junction of the roads to Inchy and Briastre. Following the latter for a little way, I decided to approach the river, but, on attempting to debouch from a gap in a hedge, we were met by a sniper's bullet. Taking cover behind a tree, we indulged in a heated argument, Evans declaring that it was a German bullet meant for us, I that it was merely a stray. There was not a soul in sight to give us information on the whereabouts of our front line.

We decided not to put the matter to the test, and we regained the road, whence we scanned the country, endeavouring to make out where our men were. Despite the thickness of the atmosphere, we could see many men, but the grey and the khaki seemed to be inextricably mingled: afterwards we learned that it was due to our men employing German prisoners as stretcher-bearers behind our line.

Evans considered the whole thing a hare-brained undertaking, but I decided to go on and find out what was happening. Proceeding along the Briastre road, we fell in with a company of stretcher-bearers, English and German, and with them we struck off towards the river. From them we learned that, though this (the left) flank had gone well forward in touch with a battalion of the 37th Division – our old friends the 4th Middlesex – on our left, the enemy still held Neuvilly itself, and from the village his snipers were directing a deadly fire upon our communications across the valley and upon the flanks of our advanced and support troops on the hill beyond.

This we soon found to be true enough. In the open space on the river bank lay many bodies, victims of the marksmen in the attics of Neuvilly. Passing swiftly across this open space, we crossed the river by a footbridge placed there for the morning's attack, and gained the cover of a small orchard. From there it was but a step along a hedge and across a ploughed field to the bank where our supports crouched.

I had originally intended pressing on to our front line, some distance ahead, but, on hearing that twelve men had been killed in the last half-hour on their way there, I desisted. The officers on the bank, who belonged to a Lancashire battalion, expressed satisfaction with the morning's barrage and directed me to the HQ of the front line battalion, which, rather to my surprise, lay much further back, in a ravine running parallel to that by which we had approached Neuvilly.

Returning across the river, we gained the headquarters. The adjutant – I think it was a battalion of the Manchester Regiment – showed us on the map the approximate line held by his men and by the Middlesex on his left. As we knew, the enemy still held Neuvilly, and the troops on the right of the village – West Riding Regiment, I think – had not been able to get beyond the railway. A direct attack was therefore to be made on the village by other troops.

Returning to the battery in time for lunch, I reported all this to Brigade HQ. In the afternoon, however, the situation changed considerably. Attacking our advanced troops in front and flank, the enemy pressed them back across the river, so that by nightfall we held nothing on the east bank of the Selle except a single post in the bank where our supports had been.

After this things became quieter, though well to our left fighting continued. The 21st Division was still at rest, and we were still covering the 17th Division, and were under their Divisional Artillery HQ. The front was, on the whole, quiet, though we fired away a good bit of ammunition on 'harassing' fire. My favourite target was the valley in front of Ovillers. I could not see into it, but it seemed probable that it sheltered some of his field batteries. Our firing on it produced much retaliation, the enemy bombarding our position heavily. In thirty-six hours we had at least 400 rounds on the position, and on the 13th one man was killed, and the orderly's horse.

All this time we had been without camouflage, having had to hand ours over to batteries of the 2nd Division on leaving the Cambrai sector. On the 14th, however, we received six large camouflage nets, and we spent the next day setting them up against a hedge on the Inchy road. Evans had the largest share in selecting and constructing the position.

When the new position was complete, we moved into it (afternoon of the 15th), having fired a final salute of sixty rounds from our old position into our favourite valley. The enemy never found our new position, but continued to bombard our old one for two days more.

By this time Magrath had rejoined us, despite the major's efforts to get him posted to the 94th Brigade. He was up at the guns, with myself, Evans and Moody. I had sent Tomlin down to the wagon-line for a rest.

On the 17th, taking Magrath as regimental officer, I reconnoitred a position south of Viesly, in a little dip rather too close to the front line for my liking. The difficulty was that only the very bottom of this depression, a strip about 20 yards wide, was invisible to the enemy. I left Magrath up there with a party of men, who dug pits and slit-trenches in advance, while Moody went up to site and supervised the construction of the mess.

Evans and I brought the battery along at nightfall. The whole brigade and two batteries of the 17th Division lay in a long line down the valley. We put up our camouflage, dug ourselves in, and hoped for the best.

Next morning we discovered that in the fog of the previous day Moody had sited the mess in such a position that it was visible to the Bosch. At this time Moody was very deaf, and had ascertained that, if the doctors certified him as deaf, he could get himself sent down to the base. But he was unwilling to leave the battery, and uncertain what to do. We commonly referred to this certificate as his 'certificate of insanity'.

When the colonel came round with the doctor that morning, the following conversation ensued:

Colonel: 'Why on earth have you stuck your mess up here? Who did it?'
Self: 'Moody, sir. In the fog yesterday–'

Evans (from inside mess, seeing doctor but not colonel): 'Here, doc! Moody wants you to certify him insane.'
Colonel: 'Not very difficult, that, I should think, if he goes on sticking up messes in full view of the Hun.'

We told Moody of this conversation afterwards. He immediately took offence, got his certificate from the doctor, and went off to the wagon-line, the Chief of General Staff, and the base. The colonel walked round the position. Always an optimist, he was certain that this would be the last battle of the war – tomorrow's attack on Neuvilly. He made us dig our guns right in. 'It would be a pity,' he said, 'to have men killed in the last battle of the war.' Before he left, he had us all expecting to hear at any moment that hostilities had ceased.

The morrow's attack was postponed, and I took the opportunity to go down and visit the wagon-line at Bertry. The place was rather far back, but there was water there – further, Miles had a good billet and was unwilling to come further up. The horses, which had suffered considerably in the waterless desert about Flesquieres, on the Cambrai front, had fallen off considerably since I had been at the guns, and the few remounts received had been of a very poor quality. We were as badly off for horses as ever, but 'D' battery, which had lost twenty-five horses from shell-fire a few days previously, was in even more need than we.

I got back to the battery after dark, and spent most of the night working out the barrage for the morning's attack – a particularly 'curly' one, with many gaps in it. Incendiary shells were to be used to frighten the enemy and to mark the completion of each stage of the barrage. These shells are credited with ability to set fire to wet sea-weed, but it seemed unlikely that they would produce any effect on the wet grass, cabbages and plough of the German positions. In the end, we only received eleven per battery, but the batteries firing on Neuvilly itself were more liberally supplied.

The attack took place at dawn on 20 October. Contrary to expectation, the enemy retaliated very little on our valley, but such shells as he did fire fell immediately in front of our guns, one man being wounded. It had rained all night, and the rain fell heavily during the attack, but, despite these adverse conditions, and the heaviness of the ground, the infantry carried out their task with success. Not quite all the objectives were gained in the morning, and at tea-time we had to repeat the last position of the barrage – they only gave us eight minutes in which to work it out. Advancing again, the infantry finished their job.

The rain made our position very miserable, as we were on plough and in a valley. The mess was flooded out. As usual, it consisted of a wide dug-out with a deep trench running down the middle, and we slept on the sides of the trench – an arrangement which ensured dry beds and minimised digging. But now the trench was full of water, and extensive bailing operations and a reconstruction of the roof, which consisted mainly of a gun-cover, had to be undertaken before we could feed or sleep in it with any comfort.

Wounded

Amerval was captured during the night of 20/21 October. On the 21st, accompanied by Tomlin, whom I had recalled from the wagon-line when Moody left us, I went with the colonel and the other battery commanders to select positions north of Neuvilly, where some batteries of the 5th Division were already established. I soon had a position chosen and went back to lunch. During the afternoon Tomlin took up some men to dig slit-trenches, etc.

Owing to a misunderstanding at the wagon-line, the teams did not get up till long after dark. The river crossing was very bad – impracticable for six-horse teams – and this led to much delay. In the evening the colonel and Roux were wounded while chatting in the 'place' at Neuvilly, and the resulting confusion at HQ caused much delay in getting telephone lines laid out. As the result of all this, we did not get into action on our SOS lines till very late.

We spent the night quietly in a little cellar – No. 49 Hauptstrasse – which had been selected by Tomlin for a mess. The address was considered a good one, the German *'Ortokommandantur'* having lived only four doors away. There were two beds, occupied by Magrath and me: Tomlin and Evans preferred the floor.

Going up to the position next morning, I was surprised to find the whole hillside thick with batteries, which had come into action around us during the night. 'A' and 'C' were just in front.

It rained hard all day. In the afternoon the battery commanders assembled at 'A' battery's position, and Major White – now commanding the brigade – gave us the orders for the morrow's attack. Ovillers was our first objective, Vendegies our second, and then, if all went well, the 62nd Infantry Brigade (passing through the 64th and 110th, which would have advanced as far as Vendegies) would continue the advance as far as they could. A complete breakthrough was hoped for: for the first time in three years, no limits were laid down.

It was very dark when I got away, but I managed to register the guns on Ovillers church. Firing on villages was not encouraged, as many of them contained civilians, and (more important) undamaged houses were better staff billets than half-ruined ones.

The barrage was to be fixed in three parts with long intervals between, each section being on a different line. Shrapnel was to be used, and many different angles of sight were required owing to the undulating nature of the ground. Under these circumstances, though I started working it out at 6 p.m. – or 18.00 hours as it was now termed – and paused only one short while for dinner, I was still hard at it at midnight, despite invaluable help by Evans, who, as on the last occasion, stayed up with me all night and relieved me of the most irritating part of the work, the reading of the contours on the map and the calculation of the varying angles of sight. I sent him to bed at midnight, intending to rest for a few moments as soon as I should have completed the fifteen barrage-tables necessary – one for each of the three sections of the barrage for each of five guns. Our sixth gun was at the Army Ordnance Department workshops, the bore having been worn by much firing.

However, I got no sleep at all that night as there was so much firing going on around us, and Harrington – acting adjutant since Martin had gone sick that morning – kept ringing me up to find out where it was.

The barrage started at 1 a.m., and the last of the three sections was concluded about 8 o'clock. The rate during the first and third sections, covering respectively the attacks on Ovillers and Vendegies, was 'intense', i.e. four rounds per gun per minute, maintained in one case for an hour. The guns failed to keep up the rate in the first section, and I had to give the Nos 1 a severe 'telling-off', after which there was no more trouble in that respect. Contrary to our expectations, the enemy did not reply on our area at all, though about a score of his aeroplanes had flown low over our positions the evening before and could not have failed to see us.

The infantry were successful in taking the two villages, but did not get far beyond Vendegies. The 7th Leicesters were caught by the enemy's shell-fire while forming up in a sunken road, and were almost completely wiped out. The 6th Leicesters, however, took both their own objectives and those of the unfortunate 7th. As a result of this day's work, the 21st Division was mentioned in the Commander-in-Chief's dispatches for the seventh time.

I had the teams up as soon as the barrage was over, but we did not receive orders to go forward for an hour or more. In the end we were told to proceed to a position of readiness between Amerval and Ovillers. Accompanied by Evans, I went on ahead. On the way we met the general, who was furious at the delay: but afterwards he apologised to White, as he found that he had himself omitted to issue orders that we were to advance as soon as the barrage ended. The 94th Brigade had already gone forward, having supplied the 'infantry batteries'.

There is a time in every battle when the artillery have completed their barrage time-table and remain ignorant as to the whereabouts and requirements of the infantry. If the battle fluctuates and the enemy's shell-fire is intense, so that few runners get back from the leading infantry, this period of uncertainty is liable to be a long one. Many systems have been devised to minimise it – FOOs going forward with telephone lines, for instance, as on the Somme, or with pigeons, as at Ypres. The one in vogue on the Selle was that of 'infantry batteries', a system which ensured that, though the leading infantry might be unable to make their requirements known to the bulk of the artillery covering them, they would yet have at their immediate disposal enough guns to deal with any ordinary obstacle.

Thus, when we arrived at Amerval, we found that, for the present, we were not required, as the infantry were going forward with the guns detailed as 'infantry batteries', the horses having been watered and fed, and the men having dinner.

In the afternoon we received orders to go forward and come into action north-east of Ovillers. Evans and I went on ahead, and selected a position, and Roberts – acting as battery captain while Miles was on leave – and Tomlin brought the battery up, the former afterwards taking the teams back to a wagon-line near Amerval.

At Neuvilly we had been in action on the ground swept by our barrage on the 20th: at Ovillers we came into action in the evening on the ground swept by our barrage of the same morning. At

Neuvilly we had found that our barrage had been tremendously effective: the ground was pocked with shell-holes and strewn with dead Germans, killed by shell-fire – and with many of our men, killed by the machine gun bullets of such Germans as survived our barrage. Here at Ovillers there were fewer shell-holes, as the proportion of HE used had been smaller and we had been specially ordered to burst our shrapnel high – only 20 per cent on graze instead of the 50 per cent or 70 per cent which we had learned at artillery schools to be the correct proportion. Also, there were very few dead Germans.

I walked up to the crest in front in the hope of registering the guns, but found the fog too thick. Above the Bois-le-Duc I found a German field-gun, standing in a shallow pit in the fields, facing Ovillers, and some frail dug-outs near it. It was of the older pattern and the bore was somewhat worn: from its history sheet I found that it had fired 16,900 rounds.

We were all very tired that night: none of us had had much sleep the night before, and I had had none at all. Having supped, we retired to rest in a shallow hole, roofed with a 'gun-cover', the time being 6.20 p.m. But I was not destined to get much rest: nine times that night I was awakened by orderlies or by the telephone. Soon after we had gone to bed White rang up, and we received orders to get the teams up and reconnoitre positions beyond Vendegies. No sooner had I sent off an orderly to fetch the teams than that order was cancelled, and I had to send another to put them off. A little while later we received our SOS lines, which ran through the very valley which we had been told to occupy, which, it became plain, was in advance of our own outposts! And so it went on.

The *piece de resistance* arrived at 3 a.m., in the form of orders for an attack at 4.30 a.m. Two brigades – the 62nd and the 64th – were to start the attack and to take Poix-du-Nord, after which the 110th Brigade was to pass through them and to continue the advance until held up. A barrage was to be put down, but that did not concern me, as I was detailed as 'infantry battery' to the 64th Brigade and the 1st Wilts (110th Brigade). I had to be in action east of Poix-du-Nord by 5.30 a.m.

The 64th Brigade was to attack with two battalions, the 9th KOYLI on the left and the 15th Durham Light Infantry on the right. When these battalions had reached their objectives, the 1st Wilts would pass through them and continue the advance as far as possible. I was to supply two guns to each battalion. I therefore detailed Evans with the centre section to work with the 15th Durham Light Infantry, and Magrath with the right section to work with the 9th KOYLI, and with the 1st Wilts when they passed through. The authorities had realised that we had not enough horses to pull six guns over the rain-sodden ploughed land, and had authorised me to keep only two sections in action.

I sent for the teams as soon as I got the orders but, owing to the state of the tracks and the press of traffic on the roads, they did not arrive until after 5 o'clock, and then, owing to a mistake at the wagon-line, not all of the officers' and staff's horses arrived which had been ordered, but only those detailed for the move of the night before, which was subsequently cancelled. It was perhaps as well that my horse did not come up, as he would never have faced the shell-fire which we encountered, which did not appear in the least to agitate the beast I rode.

It struck me that, as, of course, there was no continuous front line, there was every likelihood of our walking into the enemy, so I left Tomlin, as the most responsible of the subalterns, to bring the battery on, and went forward myself to select a position and to arrange communications, etc., with the battalions whom we were to support, accompanied by Evans (regimental officer), Bombardier Veazey (director-man), and Cpl Batters.

We rode down to the Château de la Bois du Duc, below Vendegies, where I expected to find 64th Brigade HQ. The place had been captured the day before, and with it a German battalion commander, who had delayed his escape until the last moment and then found that his retreat was barred by the moat. 62nd Brigade HQ was there, and they told me that the people I sought were not yet up, but would shortly be established in Vendegies. So I decided to press on and get in touch with the battalion commanders.

Vendegies was being heavily shelled as we passed through it, and as we left the village a 'whizz-bang' burst on graze a yard or two from Evans, who was riding on my right, sending his horse off at a canter. We rode fast over the wet roads, and came out on the crest above Poix-du-Nord without seeing a soul. There was a thick ground-mist, and we thought it possible that we had passed through our leading troops without seeing them. Against Evans' advice, however, I decided to push on mounted, having arranged that, should we by any mischance run into the enemy, anyone of us who survived would go back and warn the battery, rather than attempt to fight, as our lives were of less importance than the safety of the battery.

Thinking I saw a man in a small orchard on our left, I turned in that direction. My man turned out to be only a stump, but, beyond him, Evans descried men lying on the ground with their rifles pointed at us, only about 20 yards off. Fortunately at this moment they perceived that we were Englishmen, and held their fire – they were men of the 1st East Yorks, who were moving forward in support of the 9th KOYLI, and they had mistaken us for a German cavalry patrol. Had we not turned aside into the orchard, they would probably have engaged us at 100 yards' range as we trotted along the road, and then this history might never have been written.

Returning to the road, we went down into Poix-du-Nord. At the entrance to the village we met a detachment of the Cameronians (33rd Division), who had strayed far out of their own area. Riding briskly up the main street, we overtook the 9th KOYLI, and rode up to the head of the battalion, where we found Lt-Col Greenwood, clad in a macintosh, leading his men. For his services at the head of his battalion on this and the previous day, Col Greenwood subsequently received the Victoria Cross.

I showed the colonel on the map the position in which I proposed to put my guns, and arranged that, should he require anything, he should communicate with the section commander by runner. It was fortunate that no Bosch perceived us as we sat there on our horses, chatting with Col Greenwood and waving maps about right in front of the leading battalion, with the foremost troops – a vanguard of a dozen men – visible a score of yards ahead. Behind us some German snipers had been dragged out of the houses, and danced around in front of the muzzles of our men's' rifles, with chalk-white faces and hands held up.

We rode back through Poix-du-Nord and posted Cpl Batters at the entrance to the village, with written instructions to Tomlin not to bring the battery in until he heard from us that the village had been completely 'mopped-up', as I did not wish to risk the battery in the streets until I was assured that no German snipers remained in the houses.

The rest of us rode towards the position which I intended to occupy. Our second ride through the village was a triumphal progress. We were the first mounted men in the village, and the civilians, who were beginning to venture forth from their cellars, greeted us with cheers, offering us biscuits, flowers, and apples. Turning to the right, we overtook the 15th Durham Light Infantry, and rode to the head of the battalion, hoping to find their colonel. We did not find him, and, as we left the village, we got clear ahead in front of the battalion, and were just approaching our intended position when, all of a sudden, a shower of 'whizz-bangs' descended on us, bursting on graze all round us. They had been fired from such close range that we had not heard them coming until we found ourselves in the midst of them.

Bombardier Veazey's horse had its leg broken. Hastily dismounting, he unstrapped the director, while I prepared to shoot the horse. At that moment another 'crash' of 'whizz-bangs' fell on us, two pieces entering Evans' horse in front of the girth, and one piece passing through my leg. By this time the infantry had all taken cover: no one was visible. I packed Evans and Bombardier Veazey, with the two horses, off under cover, and hobbled down the road after them. It was my intention to disregard my wound and to carry on until the battery came up; but the heavy nature of the ground, which clung to my foot and caused me great pain at every step, deterred me.

As I leant against a barn resting, some French women appeared from a farm-house which I had supposed deserted, and helped me into the kitchen. They seated me in an armchair before the fire, regaled me on coffee, biscuits, and some exceedingly nasty liquid in a liqueur glass, and bound up my leg with my field dressing.

One of the men who was present went out and fetched Evans, to whom I handed over all the orders, etc., in my possession. He selected a position, and we sent Bombardier Veazey off on the only sound horse which remained to bring the battery up. All this had delayed matters considerably, and Col Greenwood's first request for support arrived before the battery came up. Twelve Bosch field guns, of which he gave us the map location, were holding up the advance of his battalion, and he wanted us to drive them away – rather a formidable task for the two guns detailed to support the KOYLI.

[According to the *Official War History*, it was ordered that no fire was to be directed on Poix-du-Nord as there were many French civilians there – 2,600 as it turned out. The village was 'passed through' at 8 a.m. on 24 October. A fortnight later, on 11 November, the guns fell silent: the war was over.]

LIST OF ACRONYMS

CRA: Commander Royal Artillery
CRE: Chief Royal Engineer
DAC: Divisional Artillery/Ammunition Column
FOO: Forward Observation Officer
GOC: General Officer Commanding
GS: General Service
HE: High-Explosive
KOYLI: King's Own Yorkshire Light Infantry
NCO: Non-commissioned officer
OC: Officer Commanding
OP: Observation Post
QMS: Quartermaster Sergeant
RFA: Royal Field Artillery

Also available from Amberley Publishing

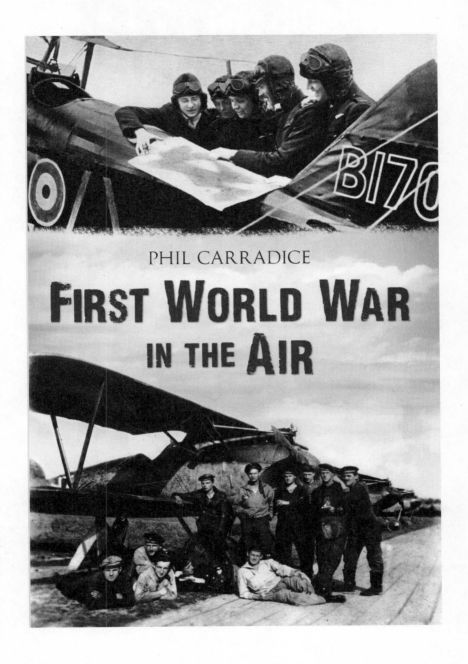

PHIL CARRADICE

FIRST WORLD WAR
IN THE AIR